DON'T Make Your Cover Letters Crash & Burn

Follow these guidelines for flameproof cover letters:

1. **Use white or off-white paper, not a weird color.**
   Printing your cover letter on cherry pop stationery overshadows your message. White or ivory paper works best. Quality rag-content paper counts for human eyes; paper quality doesn't matter for computer scanning.

2. **Start off with an original opening statement, not the basic, everyday: "Enclosed please find my resume — "**
   Find something to say that sets you above the others.

3. **Describe yourself in the first, not the third, person.**
   If you describe yourself in a narrative and use language like "Mr. Jones" achieved this or that, you will sound pompous. And we all know that Pompous Is As Pompous Does. When you speak of yourself, use the first person — I.

4. **Sound skilled and confident, not desperate.**
   Employers hire not on the basis of compassion, but for the benefits you bring to the job.

5. **Write from strength, not shortcomings.**
   Chances are that the reader will not be a member of the clergy to whom you are obliged to confess your sins. Accent your strengths.

6. **Clean up your act.**
   Typos, not signing your name, and not including your resume (if you intend to enclose one) are oversights that reek of carelessness. Carelessness leads to joblessness.

7. **Be professional, not cute.**
   Unless you're good at humor — *really good* — resist the temptation to use cutesy phrases, gags, or amusing anecdotes. If you're lucky, fun and games can come later.

8. **Give up enclosing photos or personal descriptions.**
   Unless you are going into acting, modeling, or some other performance art, do not send pictures of yourself. Keep your physical appearance a surprise for the interview.

9. **Show intent to follow up.**
   It's easier for employers to ignore you if you show no intention of calling them.

10. **Make no promises you can't keep.**
    Be able to actually do what you can say you can do. Wildly overselling yourself is a time bomb. If you fib, remember to turn out the lights on your way out the door.

BUSINESS AND
GENERAL
REFERENCE
BOOK SERIES
FROM IDG

Cover Letters For Dummies™

Quick Reference Card

DO Make Your Cover Letters RedHot News

These tips can make your cover letters too hot to turn down.

1. **Address your letters to individuals. Use names.**
   Make an intense effort to find the name and correct job title and address of the human being who will receive your letter.

2. **Name-drop early in the letter.**
   The Number One door opener is the name of a person the reader knows. Struggle to find a connection.

3. **State your objective in the first paragraph.**
   The employer is asking, "Why are you sending me this letter?" Answer the question as soon as possible.

4. **Emphasize your skills and quantify your relevant accomplishments.**
   Showcase your skills — the more you name, the better your chances of a new job. Cite your past accomplishments. Measure them in some way — numbers, dollars, or percentages.

5. **Keep your letter focused on the employer.**
   A me-me-me letter puts you out-out-out of the running. Focus on how you meet the employer's needs, not vice versa.

6. **Research companies and reflect findings in your letter.**
   Businesses not only are getting fussier about hiring good workers, they want their good workers to hit the floor running. Exhibiting knowledge of the company and its mission shows you're a fast starter.

7. **Establish your credibility by using industry-specific terms.**
   Using industry terminology demonstrates you know your stuff and that you belong.

8. **Limit your letter to one page.**
   The reader may have hundreds of letters to plow through. Get it said on one page — unless you're using a cover-letter-and-resume combo.

9. **Be friendly.**
   Show personality. Mention prior meetings with the reader or some fact connected to the target organization. Be complimentary.

10. **Make your letter easy to read.**
    White space is royal. Leave margins at least 1" wide. Choose sharp, simple, clean typefaces for your letter and strive for a good visual organization.

IDG BOOKS WORLDWIDE™

...For Dummies: Bestselling Book Series for Beginners

Praise, Praise, Praise For Joyce Lain Kennedy

"Books by Ms. Kennedy are what got me started along the path of careers in education. Another individual has been converted by your books."

—Patty McLarty, Reader, Gary, Indiana.

"Joyce Lain Kennedy's distinguished career in occupational information has placed her leaps and bounds ahead of the rest."

—Bob Calvert, Publisher, *Career News*

"Joyce Lain Kennedy has led the way in showing how technology has contributed an entirely new dimension to the job search. Her thorough knowledge of the basics lays a solid foundation for any beginner."

—David Rouse, *Booklist*

"Joyce's ability to translate computer jargon into English for the non-techie has helped me and my non-technical friends relate to that entirely new dimension."

—Judith Carbone, Career Development Center, George Mason University

"Joyce Kennedy is at the top of her field."

—John D. Erdlen, CEO, Strategic Outsourcing Inc.

"Joyce Lain Kennedy's expansive knowledge of the job search arena enables her to reach both the novice and experienced job-seeker. Truly she is the dean of careers journalists."

—Susan Estrada, CEO, Aldea Communications, Inc.

"Joyce's extraordinary awareness of every nook and cranny of career success has gained her the creditability of being a career guide guru."

—Dr. Kenneth B. Hoyt, Distinguished Professor, Kansas State University

More Praise For Joyce Lain Kennedy

"Joyce Lain Kennedy's career knowledge is the answer to any job-seeker's prayers."

—J. Herbert Wise, Executive Recruiter, Dallas, Texas

"If all new college graduates had a Joyce Lain Kennedy to guide them through their job search, there certainly would be fewer unfocused, frazzled, jobless people."

—Dr. Drema K. Howard, Director, Career Resource Center, University of South Florida

"Job search can be as you stated lonely but reading your articles has helped to keep me on the move."

—Dolores Bush, Reader, Garland, Texas

"Your articles are always interesting and very informative. You provide a valuable service to the unhappily employed and the unemployed. We're glad you're there to help."

—Joyce E. Bernotas, Reader, Bradenton, Florida

"I read Joyce's columns religiously every week. It's what keeps me motivated to keep trying harder to succeed.

—John J. Smith, Reader, Cleveland Heights, Ohio

"I have read many books and articles about 'how to,' 'what to,' and 'why not to,' but none seem to be as insightful and logical as yours."

—Peter Lamberton, Reader, E. Providence, Rhode Island

 ™

BUSINESS AND GENERAL REFERENCE BOOK SERIES FROM IDG

References for the Rest of Us! ™

Do you find that traditional reference books are overloaded with technical details and advice you'll never use? Do you postpone important life decisions because you just don't want to deal with them? Then our *. . .For Dummies*™ business and general reference book series is for you.

. . .For Dummies business and general reference books are written for those frustrated and hard-working souls who know they aren't dumb, but find that the myriad of personal and business issues and the accompanying horror stories make them feel helpless. *. . .For Dummies* books use a lighthearted approach, a down-to-earth style, and even cartoons and humorous icons to diffuse fears and build confidence. Lighthearted but not lightweight, these books are perfect survival guides to solve your everyday personal and business problems.

> *"More than a publishing phenomenon, 'Dummies' is a sign of the times."*
> — The New York Times

> *". . . you won't go wrong buying them."*
> — Walter Mossberg, Wall Street Journal, on IDG's ...For Dummies™ books

> *"A world of detailed and authoritative information is packed into them..."*
> — U.S. News and World Report

Already, hundreds of thousands of satisfied readers agree. They have made *...For Dummies* the #1 introductory level computer book series and a best-selling business book series. They have written asking for more. So, if you're looking for the best and easiest way to learn about business and other general reference topics, look to *...For Dummies* to give you a helping hand.

COVER LETTERS FOR DUMMIES™

COVER LETTERS FOR DUMMIES™

by Joyce Lain Kennedy

IDG
BOOKS
WORLDWIDE

IDG Books Worldwide, Inc.
An International Data Group Company

Foster City, CA ◆ Chicago, IL ◆ Indianapolis, IN ◆ Braintree, MA ◆ Southlake, TX

Cover Letters For Dummies™

Published by
IDG Books Worldwide, Inc.
An International Data Group Company
919 E. Hillsdale Blvd.
Suite 400
Foster City, CA 94404

Library of Congress Catalog Card No.: 96-75759

ISBN: 1-56884-395-X

Printed in the United States of America

10 9 8 7 6 5 4 3 2 1

1B/QS/QV/ZW/IN

Distributed in the United States by IDG Books Worldwide, Inc.

Distributed by Macmillan Canada for Canada; by Computer and Technical Books for the Caribbean Basin; by Contemporanea de Ediciones for Venezuela; by Distribuidora Cuspide for Argentina; by CITEC for Brazil; by Ediciones ZETA S.C.R. Ltda. for Peru; by Editorial Limusa SA for Mexico; by Transworld Publishers Limited in the United Kingdom and Europe; by Al-Maiman Publishers & Distributors for Saudi Arabia; by Simron Pty. Ltd. for South Africa; by IDG Communications (HK) Ltd. for Hong Kong; by Toppan Company Ltd. for Japan; by Addison Wesley Publishing Company for Korea; by Longman Singapore Publishers Ltd. for Singapore, Malaysia, Thailand, and Indonesia; by Unalis Corporation for Taiwan; by WS Computer Publishing Company, Inc. for the Philippines; by WoodsLane Pty. Ltd. for Australia; by WoodsLane Enterprises Ltd. for New Zealand.

For general information on IDG Books Worldwide's books in the U.S., please call our Consumer Customer Service department at 800-762-2974. For reseller information, including discounts and premium sales, please call our Reseller Customer Service department at 800-434-3422.

For information on where to purchase IDG Books Worldwide's books outside the U.S., contact IDG Books Worldwide at 415-655-3021 or fax 415-655-3295.

For information on translations, contact Marc Jeffrey Mikulich, Director, Foreign & Subsidiary Rights, at IDG Books Worldwide, 415-655-3018 or fax 415-655-3295.

For sales inquiries and special prices for bulk quantities, write to the address above or call IDG Books Worldwide at 415-655-3200.

For information on using IDG Books Worldwide's books in the classroom, or ordering examination copies, contact the Education Office at 800-434-2086 or fax 817-251-8174.

For authorization to photocopy items for corporate, personal, or educational use, please contact Copyright Clearance Center, 222 Rosewood Drive, Danvers, MA 01923, or fax 508-750-4470.

 is a trademark under exclusive license to IDG Books Worldwide, Inc., from International Data Group, Inc.

About the Author

Joyce Lain Kennedy

Joyce Lain Kennedy is the author of the *Los Angeles Times* Syndicate's column **CAREERS**, now in its 27th year and appearing in more than 100 newspapers.

Her twice weekly column is carried in the *St. Louis Post-Dispatch*, *The L.A. Times*, the *Dallas Morning News*, the *Seattle Times*, the *Louisville Courier Journal*, *Tulsa World*, and more.

Recognized as America's favorite careers journalist, Kennedy has received more than three million reader letters. In her column, she has answered in excess of 3,900 queries from readers.

Kennedy's wise counsel about job and career development addresses universal problems experienced by most working people — problems ranging from dealing with demotion to celebrating or coping with defining career moments. First to report on many new technologies and trends, Kennedy advises job seekers to relearn many strategies and tactics to prosper in a distinctly new job market.

She is the author or senior author of four books, including *Joyce Lain Kennedy's Career Book* (VGM Career Horizons) and *Electronic Job Search Revolution*, *Electronic Resume Revolution*, and *Hook Up, Get Hired! The Internet Job Search Revolution* (the last three published by John Wiley). The last three books are groundbreaking works for the new technology that's bringing people and jobs together.

Cover Letters For Dummies is one of an initial trio of books by Kennedy published under the wildly popular *. . .For Dummies* imprint: *Resumes For Dummies*, *Cover Letters For Dummies*, and *Job Interviews For Dummies*.

Writing from Carlsbad, California, a San Diego suburb, the dean of careers columnist is a graduate of Washington University in St. Louis. Her e-mail address is jlk@sunfeatures.com.

Welcome to the world of IDG Books Worldwide.

IDG Books Worldwide, Inc., is a subsidiary of International Data Group, the world's largest publisher of computer-related information and the leading global provider of information services on information technology. IDG was founded more than 25 years ago and now employs more than 7,700 people worldwide. IDG publishes more than 250 computer publications in 67 countries (see listing below). More than 70 million people read one or more IDG publications each month.

Launched in 1990, IDG Books Worldwide is today the #1 publisher of best-selling computer books in the United States. We are proud to have received 8 awards from the Computer Press Association in recognition of editorial excellence and three from Computer Currents' First Annual Readers' Choice Awards, and our best-selling ...*For Dummies*® series has more than 19 million copies in print with translations in 28 languages. IDG Books Worldwide, through a joint venture with IDG's Hi-Tech Beijing, became the first U.S. publisher to publish a computer book in the People's Republic of China. In record time, IDG Books Worldwide has become the first choice for millions of readers around the world who want to learn how to better manage their businesses.

Our mission is simple: Every one of our books is designed to bring extra value and skill-building instructions to the reader. Our books are written by experts who understand and care about our readers. The knowledge base of our editorial staff comes from years of experience in publishing, education, and journalism — experience which we use to produce books for the '90s. In short, we care about books, so we attract the best people. We devote special attention to details such as audience, interior design, use of icons, and illustrations. And because we use an efficient process of authoring, editing, and desktop publishing our books electronically, we can spend more time ensuring superior content and spend less time on the technicalities of making books.

You can count on our commitment to deliver high-quality books at competitive prices on topics you want to read about. At IDG Books Worldwide, we continue in the IDG tradition of delivering quality for more than 25 years. You'll find no better book on a subject than one from IDG Books Worldwide.

John J. Kilcullen

John Kilcullen
President and CEO
IDG Books Worldwide, Inc.

IDG Books Worldwide, Inc., is a subsidiary of International Data Group, the world's largest publisher of computer-related information and the leading global provider of information services on information technology. International Data Group publishes over 250 computer publications in 67 countries. Seventy million people read one or more International Data Group publications each month. International Data Group's publications include: **ARGENTINA:** Computerworld Argentina, GamePro, Infoworld, PC World Argentina; **AUSTRALIA:** Australian Macworld, Client/Server Journal, Computer Living, Computerworld, Digital News, Network World, PC World, Publishing Essentials, Reseller; **AUSTRIA:** Computerwelt, PC TEST; **BELARUS:** PC World Belarus; **BELGIUM:** Data News; **BRAZIL:** Annuário de Informática, Computerworld Brazil, Connections, Super Game Power, Macworld, PC World Brazil, Publish Brazil, SUPERGAME; **BULGARIA:** Computerworld Bulgaria, Networkworld/Bulgaria, PC & MacWorld Bulgaria; **CANADA:** CIO Canada, ComputerWorld Canada, InfoCanada, Network World Canada, Reseller World; **CHILE:** Computerworld Chile, GamePro, PC World Chile; **COLUMBIA:** Computerworld Colombia, GamePro, PC World Colombia; **COSTA RICA:** PC World Costa Rica/Nicaragua; **THE CZECH AND SLOVAK REPUBLICS:** Computerworld Czechoslovakia, Elektronika Czechoslovakia, PC World Czechoslovakia; **DENMARK:** Communications World, Computerworld Danmark, Macworld Danmark, PC World Danmark, PC World Danmark Supplements, TECH World; **DOMINICAN REPUBLIC:** PC World Republica Dominicana; **ECUADOR:** PC World Ecuador, GamePro; **EGYPT:** Computerworld Middle East, PC World Middle East; **EL SALVADOR:** PC World Centro America; **FINLAND:** MikroPC, Tietoverkko, Tietoviikko; **FRANCE:** Distributique, Golden, Info PC, Le Guide du Monde Informatique, Le Monde Informatique, Reseaux & Telecoms; **GERMANY:** Computer Business, Computerwoche, Computerwoche Extra, Computerwoche Focus, Electronic Entertainment, GamePro, I/M Information Management, Macwelt, PC Welt; **GREECE:** GamePro, Macworld & Publish; **GUATEMALA:** PC World Centro America; **HONDURAS:** PC World Centro America; **HONG KONG:** Computerworld Hong Kong, PCWorld Hong Kong, Publish in Asia; **HUNGARY:** ABCD CD-ROM, Computerworld Szamitastechnika, PC & Mac World Hungary, PC-X Magazine; **INDIA:** Computerworld India, PC World India, Publish in Asia; **INDONESIA:** InfoKomputer PC World, Komputek Computerworld, Publish in Asia; **IRELAND:** ComputerScope, PC Live!; **ISRAEL:** PC World 32 BIT, People & Computers; **ITALY:** Computerworld Italia, Computerworld Italia Special Editions, Lotus Italia, Macworld Italia, Networking Italia, PC Shopping, PC World Italia, PC World/Walt Disney; **JAPAN:** Macworld Japan, Nikkei Personal Computing, SunWorld Japan, Windows World Japan; **KENYA:** East African Computer News; **KOREA:** Hi-Tech Information/Computerworld, Macworld Korea, PC World Korea; **MACEDONIA:** PC World Macedonia; **MALAYSIA:** Computerworld Malaysia, PC World Malaysia, Publish in Asia; **MEXICO:** Computerworld Mexico, GamePro, Macworld, PC World Mexico; **MYANMAR:** PC World Myanmar; **NETHERLANDS:** Computable, Computer! Totaal, LAN Magazine, Macworld, Net Magazine; **NEW ZEALAND:** Computer Buyer, Computerworld New Zealand, MTB, Network World, PC World New Zealand; **NICARAGUA:** PC World Costa Rica/Nicaragua; **NIGERIA:** PC World Africa; **NORWAY:** Computerworld Norge, Computerworld Privat, CW Rapport Klient/Tjener, CW Rapport Nettverk & Telecom, CW Rapport Offentlig Sektor, IDG's KURSGUIDE, Macworld Norge, Multimedia World, PC World Ekspress, PC World Nettverk, PC World Norge, PC World's Produktguide, Windows Spesial; **PAKISTAN:** Computerworld Pakistan, PC World Pakistan; **PANAMA:** GamePro, PC World Panama; **PARAGUAY:** PC World Paraguay; **P. R. OF CHINA:** China Computerworld, China Infoworld, Computer & Communication, Electronic Product World, Electronics Today, Game Camp, PC World China, Popular Computer Week, Software World, Telecom Product World; **PERU:** Computerworld Peru, GamePro, PC World Profesional Peru, PC World Peru; **POLAND:** Computerworld Poland, Computerworld Special Report, Macworld, Networld, PC World Komputer; **PHILIPPINES:** Computerworld Philippines, PC Digest, Publish in Asia; **PORTUGAL:** Cerebro/PC World, Correio Informático/Computerworld, Mac•In/PC•In Portugal; **PUERTO RICO:** PC World Puerto Rico; **ROMANIA:** Computerworld Romania, PC World Romania, Telecom Romania; **RUSSIA:** Computerworld Rossiya, Network World Russia, PC World Russia; **SINGAPORE:** Computerworld Singapore, PC World Singapore, Publish in Asia; **SLOVENIA:** MONITOR; **SOUTH AFRICA:** Computing S.A., Network World S.A., Software World; **SPAIN:** Computerworld España, COMUNICACIONES WORLD, Dealer World, Macworld España, PC World España; **SWEDEN:** CAP&Design, Computer Sweden, Corporate Computing, MacWorld, Maxi Data, MikroDatorn, Nätverk & Kommunikation, PC/Aktiv, PC World, Windows World; **SWITZERLAND:** Computerworld Schweiz, Macworld Schweiz, PCtip; **TAIWAN:** Computerworld Taiwan, Macworld Taiwan, PC World Taiwan, Publish Taiwan, Windows World; **THAILAND:** Thai Computerworld, Publish in Asia; **TURKEY:** Computerworld Monitör, MACWORLD Turkiye, PC WORLD Turkiye; **UKRAINE:** Computerworld Kiev, Computers & Software Magazine, PC World Ukraine; **UNITED KINGDOM:** Acorn User, Amiga Action, Amiga Computing, Amiga, Appletalk, CD Powerplay, CD-ROM Now, Computing, Connexion, GamePro, Lotus Magazine, Macaction, Macworld, Open Computing, Parents and Computers, PC Home, PC Works, The WEB; **UNITED STATES:** Cable in the Classroom, CD Review, CIO Magazine, Computerworld, Computerworld Client/Server Journal, Digital Video Magazine, DOS World, Electronic, InfoWorld, I-Way, Macworld, Maximize, MULTIMEDIA WORLD, Network World, PC World, PUBLISH, SWATPro Magazine, Video Event, WebMaster; **URUGUAY:** PC World Uruguay; **VENEZUELA:** Computerworld Venezuela, GamePro, PC World Venezuela; and **VIETNAM:** PC World Vietnam   10/17/95a

Publisher's Acknowledgments

We're proud of this book; send us your comments about it by using the Reader Response Card at the back of the book or by e-mailing us at feedback/dummies@idgbooks.com. Some of the people who helped bring this book to market include:

Acquisitions, Development, & Editorial

Project Editor: Kathleen M. Cox

Acquisitions Editor: Sarah Kennedy

Editors: Tamara S. Castleman, Diane L. Giangrossi

Technical Reviewer: James M. Lemke, UCLA Department of Human Resources

Editorial Manager: Kristin A. Cocks

Editorial Assistants: Constance Carlisle, Chris H. Collins, Kevin Spencer, Ann Miller

Production

Associate Project Coordinator: Regina Snyder

Layout and Graphics: Gina Scott, Angela F. Hunckler, Brett Black, Dominique DeFelice, Drew R. Moore, Anna Rohrer, M. Anne Sipahimalani, Michael Sullivan, Patricia R. Reynolds

Proofreaders: Sharon Duffy, Christine Meloy Beck, Dwight Ramsey, Carl Saff, Robert Springer

Indexer: Judy Press

General & Administrative

IDG Books Worldwide, Inc.: John Kilcullen, President & CEO, Stephen Berkowitz, COO & Publisher

Dummies, Inc.: Milissa Koloski, Executive Vice President & Publisher

Dummies Technology Press & Dummies Editorial: Diane Graves Steele, Associate Publisher; Judith A. Taylor, Brand Manager, Myra Immell, Editorial Director

Dummies Trade Press: Kathleen A. Welton, Vice President & Publisher; Stacy S. Collins, Brand Manager

IDG Books Production for Dummies Press: Beth Jenkins, Production Director; Cindy L. Phipps, Supervisor of Project Coordination; Kathie S. Schnorr, Supervisor of Page Layout; Shelley Lea, Supervisor of Graphic and Design

Dummies Packaging & Book Design: Erin McDermitt, Packaging Coordinator; Kavish+Kavish, Cover Design

◆

The publisher would like to give special thanks to Patrick J. McGovern, without whom this book would not have been possible.

◆

Acknowledgments

To all these friends and colleagues who helped with this book, **Thanks a Ton!**

At Sun Features Incorporated

Erin Barry, Editorial Associate, who wore out three word processors pulling material together to help you lift any writer's block, and travel to a better job.

David Dunmeyer, Technical Wizard, who surfed the Internet tsunamis to bring us a tidal wave of cover letter information. His Internauting was in addition to his considerable pre-publishing formatting responsibilities — the *For Dummies* production team is picky about how we writers send in manuscripts. No handwriting in the margins, can you imagine?

Muriel Turner, Office Manager Extraordinaire, and my dear pal, who monitored endless loose ends and kept us from sinking in a sea of creative juices.

Charity De Oca, Editorial Associate, a highly creative colleague whose overflowing wastebasket and dry red pens mark a job-seeker's road to perfection.

Yara Nielsenshultz, Editorial Associate, a Ms. Manners of the English language who led the grammar team to victory.

Christopher D. Lee, **Technical Associate**, Karate Black Belt, who sparred daily with our computers. They don't mess with him anymore.

Jeffrey R. Cox, Editorial Associate and resident chilimaster for RedHot cover letters. Jeff's quick wit and editing proficiency are matched only by his skill with skill-collecting (see Chapter 5).

At Large

Special thanks to

James M. Lemke, University of California, Los Angeles

and my abundant appreciation to:

Christine Abad, Hilton Hotels Corp., Beverly Hills, California

Regina Aulisio, The Aulisio Group, San Diego, California

Richard H. Beatty, Brandywine Consulting Group, author of *175 High-Impact Cover Letters,* Malvern, Pennsylvania

Sharon Canter, Manpower, Inc., Milwaukee, Wisconsin

Douglas F. Coull, Advanced Personnel Systems, Oceanside, California

John D. Erdlen, Strategic Outsourcing Inc., a division of Romac International Inc., Wellesley, Massachusetts

Betty L. Laurie, American Compensation Association, Scottsdale, Arizona

John Lucht, The Lucht Consultancy, and author of *Rites of Passage at $100,000+: The Insider's Lifetime Guide to Executive Job-Changing*, New York City

Patrick O'Leary, United Parcel Service Airlines, Louisville, Kentucky

Kathleen Ortiz, Great Western Financial Securities Corp., Los Angeles, California

Elayne Reichard, Adolph Coors Company, Golden, Colorado

Craig VonKouwenberg, The Shelbourne Group, Lancaster, Pennsylvania

Sheldon Weinhaus, Esq., Employment Attorney, St. Louis, Missouri

Contents at a Glance

Cartoons at a Glance

By Rich Tennant   Fax: 508-546-7747   E-Mail: the5wave@tiac.net

"No, I don't think including a lock of your hair is the right way to personalize your cover letter."

page 45

"Well Kid, if your resume's as good as your cover letter, you've got a place with this gang."

page 7

"Yes, Mr. Van Gogh, now that I have your ear, so to speak, let me thank you for that enticing cover letter."

page 119

page 77

"I sent my cover letter over the Internet and got 3 responses in less than a week. Unfortunately they're from 3 different continents, none of which I live on."

page 167

Table of Contents

Introduction

● ●

*Y*ou've finished your resume, and it's a masterpiece. Now what?
Even a KickButt resume (see my book *Resumes For Dummies*, from IDG
Books Worldwide, Inc.) needs a bodyguard: the cover letter — the RedHot
cover letter. Your RedHot cover letter is the wake-up call you send with your
resume, giving the recipient the burning sensation that you two should have
met yesterday. It says, "Meet me! Meet me!" The letter's main purposes are to

- ✔ Arouse the reader's interest
- ✔ Explain why you are well qualified to be hired
- ✔ Showcase your own wonderful personality
- ✔ Tell the recipient that you'll call for an appointment

Other cover letters can do some nice things for you — like make you feel
special, thicken the envelope that contains your resume, look official, or give
you a good excuse to use that handsome stationery you've been saving for a
special occasion — but those letters don't sell you like hotcakes. They're just
letters. The RedHot letter is more. It's a superlative marketing tool to prove that
you're a RedHot candidate, that you're the greatest thing since the jalapeño,
and that readers had better get you in their office before someone else does.

What Is a RedHot Cover Letter?

A RedHot cover letter is

- ✔ Hot-wired to a target job
- ✔ So intriguing that a reader makes room in a busy schedule to meet you
- ✔ An electrifying personal advertising tool that short-circuits the
  competition

A RedHot cover letter is not

- ✔ Bland and indifferent
- ✔ Littered with frozen, dry facts
- ✔ What the hiring manager's kid uses for scratch paper

Okay, so you're still a little skeptical. *RedHot* may sound slightly devilish, like you've got something up your sleeve. You do: your skills, accomplishments, and experience. Your RedHot cover letter sparks the reader's interest as a hot-poker introduction to your KickButt resume. The cover letter is your chance to personalize your resume. Here's where you make yourself into a living, breathing human being and set your accomplishments aglow. Drawing from your KickButt resume — and it had better be KickButt-class, or your cover letter may as well go to the employer solo — you spice up your data by paralleling your qualifications to those on the employer's hot list.

So you're saying to yourself, "A letter. To someone I don't know? I don't even write thank-you notes to Aunt Jane for the nice check she sends me every year for my birthday." Or maybe you haven't written anything formal since you sat up nights drafting and redrafting college research papers. Although it's a writing exercise, a cover letter is nowhere near the length of the ten-pagers you once grappled with. However, cover letters have far more relevance overall: They tell what you want to do and why you are qualified to do it.

But to Whom Do You Write?

My answer is — write to everybody! Just writing letters in response to printed advertisements is not enough in this job-hunting jungle. To begin, write letters to everyone you can think of who may have job leads or advice. Start with friends and relatives and move outward to acquaintances or old friends you haven't talked to in years. Of course, you can't limit your letter-sending only to people you know, but those people are a great tryout for the big leagues.

As you can see, *cover letter* is an umbrella term encompassing a whole slew of employment letters. Just as you write to different people, your individual letters highlight different aspects of your career or different needs in your job search.

The letters discussed in this book illustrate how to keep a hot-pepper charge burning throughout your correspondence with prospective employers.

What's in This Book

Part I, Cover Letters that Say You're a Hot Hire, tells why you need a cover letter, what kinds of cover letters exist, what myths surround cover letters, and how to break out of writer's block.

Part II, Working Out What Sizzles, presents a skills finder to help you identify where your skills fit in today's jobset, and guides you through a number of self-assessment worksheets. These worksheets are helpful in creating your resume as well.

Part III, Writing RedHot Cover Letters, shows you how your letter should look and sound; it lists tips on language, content, and image. It also includes a checklist that lets you rate your cover letter by RedHot criteria.

Part IV, A Collection of RedHot Cover Letters, gives you annotated samples of RedHot cover letters that have come across my desk. Of course, the names, addresses, and other identifying information have been changed. But you get the idea.

Part V, The Part of Tens, offers sure-hire tips for answering job ads, working with recruiters, avoiding the salary question, and some do's and don'ts for creating cover letters too hot to turn down.

And some problem words and ways to use them correctly are included in the **Appendix,** so you can avoid making embarrassing mistakes that could literally cost you a job.

Icons Used in This Book

One helpful feature of the *...For Dummies* series is the liberal use of cute pictures called icons that draw your attention to information too hot to ignore. These are the icons used in this book and what they signify.

These powder-keg tips will make your cover letter burn all the rest.

Pay attention to this icon so you don't come across as a clueless beginner, even if you are one.

This icon highlights tips for the individual who's been around the business block but whose experience may need to be fired up.

This icon notes the fundamental facts of cover letter preparation and job hunting. When you need to get down to basics, this is it.

Look here for smokin' advice from whizzes in the job-finding business.

This icon flags words of wisdom for you to brand into your memory.

This icon spotlights differences of opinion in the art of cover letter writing.

This icon alerts you to mistakes that could end up costing you a job.

Technology can overtake even the most non-nerdy of us, and electronic technology has overtaken the job-finding search. This icon highlights things that help make your resume computer-friendly.

A Time for RedHot Cover Letters

If you're still in doubt about the power of cover letters, consider this example supplied by Jim Lemke, manager of employment and human resource information systems at the University of California, Los Angeles, and a former manager of employment at Walt Disney Imagineering. He shares this delightful cover letter story:

At Disney, a job letter arrived from a young man with a simple message:

> *I want to work for Walt Disney. I am creative. My resume proves it.*

The human resource department at Disney sent back a standard software-generated response acknowledging the receipt of the resume and stating that his resume would be scanned into a database. If a suitable job opening arose, he would be contacted.

A second letter arrived from the young man. It said:

> *I don't think you understand. I really, really, really, really, really want to work for Walt Disney.*

Disney's human resource job computers sent out a second message promising to keep his resume.

Soon a third communication from the young man arrived. It was a ransom note, with letters cut from a newspaper. One ear from a mouseketeer hat was pinned to the note:

You still don't get it. I've got the mouse. I want a job.

Yes, the young man got the job. The key is that Disney hired him for his creative mind. Don't try this ploy at Bank of America, but also remember that a cover letter gives you your chance to really shine. A well-written cover letter can help make your ideal job a reality. So start writing.

Part I

Cover Letters That Say You're a Hot Hire

The 5th Wave — By Rich Tennant

"Well kid, if your resume's as good as your cover letter, you've got a place with this gang."

In this part . . .

You know that you're talented. You know that you're capable of doing any job for which you're qualified, and you know you're capable of doing the job well. So do your friends, parents, and all the other people who love you. Now all you need to do is convince that employer out there. You need a RedHot cover letter.

This part explains why a good cover letter helps you accomplish your employment goals. This part also exposes some cover letter myths and gets you on the road to your own RedHot cover letters.

Chapter 1

The RedHot Cover Letter Kick-Off

● ●

In This Chapter

▶ Why you need RedHot cover letters

▶ Overcoming writer's block

▶ How new technology affects targeting your letters

▶ Answers to cover letter questions

● ●

A resume should almost never go out alone in the world of employment. A resume needs a cover letter as a companion. Twenty-five years ago, a cover letter was strictly a transmittal message. It said: *Here's my resume* and very little else.

That was then, this is now. Today's cover letter does far more than ride shotgun for your resume. Today's cover letter is itself a marketing tool, personalized and bursting with vitality. Sometimes the letter is on paper, sometimes it's on a computer. Either way, today's cover letter offers a great chance to generate an employer's interest in interviewing you.

How great a chance? A recent study by Accountemps, a worldwide temporary staffing service for financial people, found that 60 percent of responding executives believe that when screening applicants, the cover letter is either as important as or more critical than the resume.

Perhaps you haven't yet gotten the hang of writing contemporary cover letters because you think you can't write your way out of a paper bag, let alone write a letter that will catch an employer's eye. Is that what you think — don't try because you can't write? I bet you can. And this book will prove I'm right.

All your protests add up to is the need to expend extra energy into getting your thoughts down on paper — or on a computer screen. This book is loaded with the writing aids and tips you need to do just that.

You Can Learn to Write Cover Letters

Here's the thing: RedHot cover letter writing is a *learnable skill*. It is not Pulitzer Prize writing; it is getting-you-an-interview writing. If your cover letter attracts an employer's interest, the employer will read your resume to confirm a positive first impression. (Conversely, some employers go straight to the resume and, if they like what they see, turn back to examine the other gems of information that grace the cover letter.)

Virtually anyone can learn to write effective cover letters. You *can* conquer the cover-letter challenge if you really care about improving your career.

The difference between RedHot cover letters and run-of-the-mill cover letters is

- ✔ Strong personalization
- ✔ High energy
- ✔ Relevant information
- ✔ Moderately informal
- ✔ A breath of fresh air

A cover letter with each of these qualities is RedHot! The difference in the way you write is not night and day. What sets the RedHot letters apart is a nuance of tone: greater zest, more vitality, more enticement — without extraterrestrial attempts at being clever.

Put your heart and soul into learning to write cover letters with passion! With apologies to Robert Frost: *No interest in the writer, no interest in the reader.*

In the competition of today's marketplace, you cannot afford to spend plenty of time perfecting your resume, and then throw together a routine cover letter to slap on top. Putting your cover letter on autopilot downgrades your entire self-marketing package. Think about it: your marvelous resume and the boilerplate letter — what an odd couple to send marching out to do battle for you in a scary job world.

The Advantages of RedHot Cover Letters

If you're having a little trouble in your job search (and who isn't these days?), a RedHot letter differentiates you from a mushrooming mob of qualified hunters intent on nailing the job you want. A RedHot letter gives employers their first glimpse of you and the benefits you bring. It entices employers to give your resume a good going over. By contrast, a run-of-the-mill cover letter encourages employers to keep thumbing through the stack of applicants.

More specifically, why should you bother to write a RedHot cover letter? Here are 11 good reasons.

Good first impression

A RedHot letter, as your first knock-on-the-door, grabs attention of the resume reader: *Hey you RezReader, slow down, stop, look at me!* The attention flows when you spotlight specific skills important to the reader. A RedHot letter causes the reader to look at your resume with heightened interest by answering the question in most employers' minds — *What can you do for us?*

Focus on employer

A RedHot letter focuses on the employer, in contrast to the resume that focuses on you. Psychologists are right — we all like to think about ourselves. That goes double for employers. Use words like *offer* and *contribute* over *growth potential* and *career opportunity*. A RedHot letter is a superb employment tool to address the benefits that you bring to the employer.

Matchmaking with benefits

Salespeople are told: *Customers buy benefits, not features.* Your letter personalizes your qualifications in terms of benefits and conveys them directly to a particular person. It tells the employer why you have what she wants. You stand out from the crowd by correlating your top skills, knowledge, and achievements with the employer's priorities. You can clearly state why this organization is a perfect place for you to make a contribution.

The family of job letters

Although this book title refers to cover letters, the title is something of a misnomer. This book covers the entire range of letters for job search needs, not only letters that respond to recruitment advertising and calls from executive recruiters. You'll find networking letters, broadcast letters, thank-you letters, and offer acceptance and rejection letters, as well as recommendation letters you write yourself. For the full range, see Chapters 3, 4, 11, and 12.

Up-to-speed image

A RedHot cover letter shows that you're in tune with the innovations affecting businesses today. In fast-breaking industries, employers assume new graduates have current knowledge.

Job hunters more than 15 years out of school should make a point of showing that they do not believe the way they worked yesterday is the best way to work today and tomorrow. They should mention major changes the target industry is undergoing and explain what they have done to keep pace. The cover letter is an ideal place to convey that you are on the curve as new business worlds stir.

Shows savvy

A RedHot letter demonstrates your ability to understand and fulfill a company's specific needs. It shows you are smart enough — and committed enough — to scout the company's products, services, markets, and employment needs.

Presells you

A RedHot cover letter presells your qualifications, encouraging the reader to imagine you as qualified, personable, and savvy — the type of person to spend 30 minutes of a finite lifetime checking out. A strategic letter prepares the reader to like you. A good cover letter is like having a TV show announcer warm up the audience before the star appears.

You keep control

A RedHot cover letter puts control in your hands. It sets up a reason for you to call the employer, if the employer doesn't beat you to the phone. By promising to call, when you do telephone, you can truthfully get past the gatekeeper by saying that your call is expected.

Adaptability: A practical matter

Cover letters should be personal, of course. Whenever possible, write to a person, not a company. But, for practicality, you should first develop a core cover letter.

Once the core letter is polished, your cover letter has the versatility of a basic blue suit or black dress that goes from morning until evening, with only a slight change of accessories. A core letter can be dressed up in any number of ways to address specific situations. You may develop several core cover letters — one for each career field. Write a new opening, plug in the target job specifics, and you have a whole new letter.

Career-changing bonus

It's not a magic bullet by any means, but your cover letter can be directed to help you change careers. When your most recent work experience is different than the career field you wish to enter, use your cover letter to accent your skills that best match the new field. Should you mention why you want to switch? Generally, I wouldn't; doing so just calls attention to your less-than-perfect match for the job. At times, though, it may be necessary. Suppose that you worked for four companies, each of which was sold. You might conclude your letter by saying

I am well qualified for a small company where many hats are in vogue. I gained broad experience in different environments during 19XX-19XX at four companies: A, B, C, and D. Each company was acquired, resulting in changes of management. Despite departures of key personnel, excellent references are available.

You: A three-dimensional person

With a RedHot cover letter, instead of being just a name and a set of qualifications, you come alive as a real person with benefits to offer, goals, ideas, and personality. A well-done cover letter suggests that you're knowledgeable, able, talented, and take pride in your work. By contrast, a poor or boring letter suggests that your work will be likewise.

Reveals critical thinking

A RedHot cover letter shows the employer how your mind works — how you state your position and then pull everything together in a lucid rationale. In a related evaluation, your cover letter proves you can communicate in writing — useful for sales letters, memos, and reports.

The Disadvantages of RedHot Cover Letters

There aren't any.

Many Job Hunters Have Writer's Block

Perhaps the biggest reason you're struggling with writing cover letters is that you need to rethink your career goals. You really can't do your best writing about where you want to go until you know where that is.

Even when you're certain of your direction, you may still be stuck at square one. This phenomenon is called writer's block.

One cure writers use is *freewriting*. Writing becomes a problem for some people when they try to start at the beginning. When you freewrite, take about 15 minutes to randomly scratch out your thoughts on paper or bang away at your computer keyboard. Do not slow down to organize or edit. After you've pushed your pen for the full 15 minutes, read over your work. Mark ideas, words, and phrases that you can use in your letter. You may wish to freewrite several times until your thinking ink warms up.

Another technique to stop staring at a blank page is to answer these questions. Find a friend to help you brainstorm, making notes as you go.

INSIDER HINT

Targeting a RedHot letter

No letter is so versatile that it applies perfectly to every job and reader. Readers can smell cookie-cutter cover letters, and they discount them. Putting a lot of yourself into your cover letters demonstrates your interest in gaining familiarity with specific employers and their needs. Even when you do your best, expect to fail occasionally. You cannot control an employer's likes and dislikes, sense of humor, cluelessness, or bias. Take a few chances, and never give up.

Technology has thrown a wild card into your cover letter submissions. Until electronic resume databases became common, sticking to a single job objective in your cover letter was smart when writing to an employer.

Now your objective is to be considered for more than one job if your first effort fails. Employers keep resumes for months, even years. Before they go outside the company to recruit, they search internal databases.

When you are certain (call and ask) that you are sending your resume to a company that uses a *scanning automated applicant system* (most large companies do), submit a resume and a general cover letter to the human resources department.

This *nontargeted* cover letter should focus on your general interest in obtaining a position with the company: "I've always admired the vision and accomplishments of the ABC Company. Please consider my resume for any position which you believe will be mutually beneficial."

If you have the name of the hiring manager (call and ask), send the manager a *targeted* cover letter along with your resume (make sure it is exactly the same resume), stating why you are the best candidate for the current opening. Also mention that you have concurrently transmitted a resume to the human resources department.

1. Whom do you picture reading your letter? What is that person wearing? In what environment is that person reading your letter — a well ordered office or a room that looks like a teenager's retreat?
2. Which qualities do you want to emphasize in your letter?
3. Why will your letter be interesting and important to the reader?
4. What benefits do you bring to the reader's company?
5. What special skills or talents set you apart from the competition?
6. Why do you think your employability (person- specific) skills will help you fit into a new company?
7. How are your previous jobs similar to those you now seek? If the jobs are different, what skills are the same and transferable?
8. What do you like about the company to which you are applying?

Here's a tip for people who speak better than they write but must learn to write cover letters: Audiotape your letter with a voice recorder. Ask a friend to engage in a discussion about the job. Tell the friend why you are a hot prospect to fill the job. From that tape may come sound-bite excerpts that lift your letter out of humdrum status.

Keep in mind as you embark on the process of learning to write RedHot cover letters that your first draft is probably going to be shredder-bait, but your editing and refining can fix almost anything.

No Hard and Fast Rules

Just as absolutes do not exist in resume writing, neither do they exist in cover letter creation. You won't find a "best" way to do cover letters. As University of Pennsylvania career counselor Mary Morris Heiberger says:

"If there were a best way ... all employers would have to be clones of each other, sharing identical tastes, priorities, and opinions."

Packaging and Presentation

Use a computer's word processor and laser printer to turn out a fine-looking letter. Choose standard business size (8¹/₂" x 11") paper in white or eggshell.

Aim for a letter with no warts, no typos, and clean as a whistle.

Get Ready to Write

If you want your career to take off, your cover letters had better be terrific. Take more risks, offer more surprises, find fresh ways to sell your benefits and skills. Pledge to never send out a run-of-the-mill letter again. From now on, you're in RedHot mode!

Overcoming WhatIf Worries

WhatIfs (what-if questions) are legitimate worries when writing cover letters whose solutions may not be obvious.

WhatIf Worry	Answer
WhatIf I'm responding to a recruitment ad — to whom should my cover letter be addressed?	Send your RedHot cover letter with a KickButt resume (see my book *Resumes For Dummies*) to the individual or department named in the advertisement. Follow instructions.
WhatIf the instructions say to send the letter and resume to the human resource department? That's a waste!	Not at all. New technology means that your resume will likely go into an electronic database and be stored for a long time; you may be considered for a number of open positions. In addition to following instructions, send a second RedHot cover letter to the name of the department hiring manager (your prospective boss). Say your resume is on file with HR (human resources). Get the hiring manager's name by anonymously calling, and hope to break through voice mail.
WhatIf I don't know enough about the position to write a RedHot letter?	Look up job descriptions for similar positions, and read recruitment ads in print and online. Try to make online contact with people in the target career field through Internet newsgroups and mailing lists. This step is a long shot, but try to get through on the telephone to a person who does similar work for a competitor.

WhatIf Worry	Answer
WhatIf I'm responding to an executive recruiter — do I send the same materials?	Send the same resume but change the letter (see Chapter 14). Mention that while you're very interested in this position, you would like to be considered for other jobs if this one doesn't pan out.
WhatIf I'm initiating a possible opening at a company that has not advertised one?	Research to determine who has the line authority to hire you. Send your self-marketing materials to that person. Even more effective is to meet your target at a professional meeting or find a third party whose name you can use as an introduction (see Chapter 12).

Chapter 2

Cover Letter Myths That Stop You Cold

● ●

In This Chapter
▶ Revealing myths that could make a letter drop dead
▶ Other fictions that sell your letter short

● ●

Many people think that cover letters are an optional exercise in the job-finding game. They look at the cover letter as a throw-away piece that no one pays attention to. They take short-cuts and fall for myths guaranteed to show prospective employers that you don't care enough to send your very best. Don't cut corners with your cover letters. Believing the myths that follow can kill your cover letter before it has a chance to sell your skills.

Don't Fall for These Myths

Your resume may not be resurrected if you don't protect it with a well-written cover letter. The only benefit to be achieved by these false beliefs is the one your competitors get by having you fall from job candidate status.

It's OK to send your resume without a cover letter

False! Unless you like to send your resume into other people's trash cans, make sure that a cover letter accompanies your resume. Your cover letter stamps a personality on your resume, a personality that the reader may find tough to reject out of hand.

Your cover letter summarizes your resume

False! A summary of the resume and the resume with a summary seem a little repetitive, yes? Use a cover letter to add a warm handshake to your resume and to zero in on why the employer should be interested in you. Your cover letter should put your resume in context — it should draw attention to your strengths and present nonresume material that can make the difference between you and your next closest competitor when the interviewing decision is made.

A cover letter merely introduces your resume

False! Your cover letter premarkets your resume — that's true. But your letter is also ultimately a silent force, enticing the reader to scour your resume. Some employers believe cover letters are more important than resumes when choosing candidates to interview. If your cover letter doesn't flesh out the person presented in your resume, you may never get to meet the reader face-to-face.

You can routinely use a generic greeting — "Dear Employer"

False! Imagine that your job is to screen job applicants, and every letter you read begins with *Dear Job Application Reviewer*, or in effect, *Dear Nobody*. Research your target organization until you have the name and gender of the person who will review your resume. Double-check for correct spelling and proper job titles. When you can't uncover the correct name and must rely on a generic greeting, *Dear Employer* is as good as anything. Don't assume gender and use *Gentlemen* for your salutation.

What do you do when you're answering a blind ad, and you don't know who will review your resume? If the ad gives a U.S. Postal Service box address for reply, you're in luck. Postal regulations[1] require that the postmaster of a U.S. Post Office must reveal, upon demand, the name of any person or entity renting a postal box to "solicit business." (The identity need not be revealed of individuals who rent U.S. postal boxes for personal use or of commercial boxes in commercial establishments.) You can ask a postal clerk for the name of the box holder, and then make an educated guess as to which department is hiring. Call the company's receptionist and ask if John Doe (make up a name) is the manager of that department; the receptionist may correct the name for you. Truthfully say that you are writing a letter, get the spelling down pat, and send off your RedHot cover letter properly addressed to *Dear Somebody-by-Name*.

[1]The postal regulation releasing the names of business renters of postal boxes is in the Administrative Support Manual, Reg. 352.44, Section E, #1.

Keep your cover letter really, really short — like a paragraph

False! The length of your cover letter depends not upon absolute rules of measurement, but upon the amount of content you have to convey. When the letter escorts a resume, I suggest limiting the letter to one page, with one to six paragraphs; when your letter substitutes for a resume, two to three pages is the max.

Devote one paragraph for each salient point. The short-paragraph technique maintains your letter's richness even when skimmed at transwarp speed. *Your RedHot cover letter should be just long enough to accommodate all your priority attributes and to motivate the reader to review your resume and meet with you.*

A handwritten cover letter is best — it's personal

False! Handwriting is certainly personal — but for job letters the risks are too high. What are the risks? Employers may assume you are way behind the times if you don't use a computer's word processor, or they may be unable to read your penmanship. If an employer wants a sample of your handwriting, the employer will request one. Your only handwriting should be your signature at the end, written in black or blue ink. (Colored inks like red or green are seen as unprofessional. Don't risk a job for a color statement.)

Resumes and networking are infinitely more important than cover letters in a job search

False! Finding a job is not a one-trick pony. You need the tools of marketing materials — cover letters and resumes — in your quest for job leads, which include recruitment advertising response, networking, and direct application among the most productive techniques. No one component is provably more important than the others. In a job search during the Great Downsizing of America, you need all the help you can get.

Anyone can find a job — if your cover letter isn't working, the letter is at fault

False! Your marketing materials — a cover letter or resume — can become an easy focus for your anxieties about a job search. Many of the moving parts of the employment process are frustratingly placed beyond your control: voicemail keeps you from reaching a preferred employer, job openings for your target seem to go underground, interviews fail to spark job offers.

By contrast, the preparation of a cover letter and resume is entirely under your control. When things go wrong, blaming the marketing materials is convenient (although often the blame is well placed). Consequently, job seekers often think if they can only whip their marketing materials into perfect shape, the other parts of the search will turn out favorably. The truth is, all parts of your search must be up and running.

Your cover letter gets you a job

False! According to this logic, a cherry pit gets you a cherry. A cherry pit planted in fertile soil gets you a tree and then maybe a cherry. A RedHot cover letter riding shotgun for a resume gets you an interview and then maybe a job. To succeed in your job search, you need a strategy for finding job leads (*Job Hunting For Dummies* can help) and a KickButt resume (see my book, *Resumes For Dummies,* for what puts your resume in the KickButt class), supported by a RedHot cover letter. In addition, you need marketable skills, appropriate personal qualities, interviewing strengths, and the right references. It's the total package that determines who wins the job.

The cover letter is your chance to talk about your personal life and feelings

False! Your resume talks about you; your cover letter talks about your intended employer — and how your employer can benefit from the splendid assets you offer. Describe special benefits that set you above other applicants. Rambling about personal feelings and situations in an employment letter is a blatant display of self-interest and, worse, is boring. An exception can be made when you're seeking to relocate (provided you offer to pay for the move). Many employers appreciate the desire to be near family as a reason to relocate. No need to go into your uncle's stint in the nursing home — having family in the area is enough.

Include salary history and expectations in your cover letter

False! Save the salary discussion for the interview. You can be eliminated at this stage if your salary history is considered too high, too low, or too static. Don't get into it. If an ad requests such information, write that your salary is negotiable and that you'd be happy to discuss the issue during an interview. See Chapter 16 for more information about how to handle the salary issue.

Once you send a letter, the employer carries the ball

False! No matter how terrific you are, most employers have no time for hunting you down unless they need you right this very second. Call to be sure that your letter and resume arrived. If you are sending unsolicited marketing materials, ask for an interview. If you are responding to recruitment advertising, ask if you are a match for the open position and when an appointment can be scheduled.

The never-say-die telephone strategy of years past — which requires you to doggedly call back every 10 days or two weeks — no longer works well. Companies are understaffed; interviewers are overworked. Harried interviewers resent you for breaking into their days with excessive telephone calls. Remaining connected through well-written postal letters, e-mail, and faxes that offer information the employer can use is a much better idea.

Sending your letter by courier is an attention-getter

False! Unless time is of the essence, save your money. Anyone who cares how your letter arrives usually doesn't have the power to hire you. Mail usually filters through office staffers before reaching hiring managers. Even a courier envelope that costs you a meal is likely to be opened by nonhiring hands. In many offices, however, e-mail and faxes still get the hiring manager's attention, because they often route straight to your target.

When mailing, use a standard business envelope

False! Before the dawn of electronic magic, folding a letter for a 4" x 9.5" envelope was standard. Now that your documents face a good chance of being scanned and stored by job computers, inserting your letter and resume flat and unfolded into a 10" x 13" envelope is safer. Creases from folding may damage your document's text in scanning systems. By using a larger envelope, you have a huge edge over thousands of other job seekers who don't know that their marketing materials should arrive scanner-ready.

Paper quality always has a great effect on your image

False! And True! Cover letters and resumes are read both by humans and by computers. For a finger-friendly read, paper quality counts. And the more rag content, the better.

For a computer-friendly read, the quality of paper doesn't matter at all — the finest paper becomes just another pretty electronic face. Your cover letter and resume paper should match, be white or off-white smooth paper, sized 8.5" x 11". Avoid glossy or coarse textures that can cause scanners to misread. Don't use colored paper — especially blue, green, and gray, which may scan in as shades of gray that obscure your letter's text.

Chapter 3

Action Letters That Respond to Needs

- -

In This Chapter

▶ Meeting the five-member family of responding letters

▶ Writing when you know a job opening exists

▶ Responding to recruitment ads

- -

*T*he job letter family is easier to understand if we think of the members in two main groups:

✔ Action letters that **respond** to needs

Letters in this group are written when you know a job opening exists. These are *reactive letters*.

✔ Action letters that **initiate** leads

Letters in this group are written to inquire about a possible job opening. These are *proactive letters*. You can read more about initiating letters in Chapter 4.

Also in this category are thank-you letters and other letters you are not required to write but that you initiate as a way to follow up on a possible job opening.

You can hardly believe your immense good fortune — after beating the bushes for light years, you've finally learned of a job that seems just right for you!

Perhaps you found the job in a help-wanted advertisement in a newspaper or professional journal or saw the job posted on the Internet. Perhaps you got wind of it in your networking moves or heard the job described on a job hotline. Perhaps a friend called to say a job is opening where he works. No matter how you found out about the job, you know an opening exists, and you break speed limits to reply. You want — as quickly as possible — to show your intention of becoming a candidate for the position and ask for a job interview.

As you pull up short in front of a computer, you're confronted by a sudden thought: What sort of letter shall I write that will nail this job for me?

This chapter answers that question by introducing you to five basic action letter categories — each of which can respond to specific needs of employers. They are

- **Resume letter**
- **T-letter**
- **Blind ad reply letter**
- **Employment service letter**
- **Targeted resume letter**

In the next few pages, you'll learn the concept, mission, advantages, and disadvantages of the responding letter.

Model letters that illustrate responding letters are found in Chapter 11. Any of these five types can be formidable when used to heat up your chances of being called for a meeting. This chapter offers some thoughts on which type is most likely to ignite interest in your qualifications

The Resume Letter: A Familiar Type

The resume letter is the one that escorts your resume when you respond to a recruitment ad. This letter is the one most commonly thought of when you hear the term "cover letter."

The resume letter is more than shrinkwrap for your resume, however. Another weapon in your arsenal of flame-throwing, self-marketing materials, the resume cover letter adds personality to a formal resume. In effect, your resume cover letter says:

I am highly motivated and have built a solid reputation (whether at school or at work) for tireless enthusiasm, resourcefulness, accuracy, and careful work — all essential skills for a (your occupation). Go ahead and read my resume. I'm hot stuff!

The resume letter's mission

- To get your resume read
- To turn you into a three-dimensional being

Advantages of a resume letter

- Directs the focus of your resume
- Highlights your skills

Uncovering job ads

🖊 Check out newspapers, trade and professional publications, association newsletters, job hotlines, public employment service job banks, electronic bulletin boards, newspaper help-wanted classifieds on the Internet (http://www.careerpath.com), and Internet recruitment advertising — use a search engine such as Alta Vista (http://www.altavista.com).

🖊 Skim through ads in fields outside your own — you may find yourself fitting into a new career field or fitting a new field to your career.

🖊 Not only should you apply to ads you match exactly, but to any openings for which you may be slightly over- or under-qualified. Employers often advertise for the perfect match, but adjust their requirements as applications are received. Forget this tactic if you are over- or under-qualified by a country mile.

🖊 Stay alert to companies doing major recruitment — they may only advertise some openings but actually have many others of interest to you.

🖊 Even if you're pushed for time, target specific readers with personalized letters. Employers sniff-and-trash form letters like spent socks.

🖊 Even if rejected once by a company, continue replying (with revised letters) to the company's ad as long as it runs — their human tracking systems often have a poor memory. Dynamics change when job computers enter the picture. If you know (because you've called to ask) that a computer is tracking applicants, be extremely careful about sending multiple resumes. If your letters do not seem to describe the same person with the same set of skills and other qualifications, you will raise serious questions about who you really are. Computers usually retrieve by name and telephone number. If you are determined to send wildly different resumes, change the telephone number and use initials instead of your first name.

🖊 Don't shy from blind ads. (The employer's name is not given, only a box number, or coded reference.) Your objective is to maximize every possible interview source.

🖊 The traditional advice is to apply separately for each position with the same company. One application is enough when you know the company uses a job computer to track applicants. Your resume is entered in a database, which is then searched as different positions open. For more details, see my book, *Electronic Resume Revolution* (Wiley).

Disadvantages of a cover letter

🖊 One glaring typo or error and, for this employer, your whole life could wind up as a wad of recycled paper.

🖊 Because this format is expected (conventional formatted letter plus a resume), the presentation must be outstanding or the letter risks boring the reader.

Watch for clues

Sleuth the wording of recruitment ads before writing your response letter. Pay attention to special emphasis placed on requirements, especially if they are repeated. Be certain to mention those requirements in your letter. Tipoffs to crucial requirements are preceded or followed by such demands as

(Requirement) is a plus   Is required

Desirable   Must be strongly versed in

Very desirable   Must be knowledgeable in

Must be   Should be strong in

Must be capable of   Proficiency in

Must have

The T-Letter: The New Champion

My personal favorite is the T-letter, a dynamite letter that matches point-by-point the employer's priorities with the qualifications you offer. This letter can accompany a resume, or it can be written as a targeted resume letter (described later in this chapter).

I call it the "You-want/I-have" letter because, graphically, this type makes seeing why your application deserves consideration so easy.

The T-letter can be constructed in one of two basic ways.

> ✔ The ledger layout (see Figure 3-1) is the most common. In the left column you write the employer's requirements that you find in the advertisement; across from each item, you write your qualification that meets the requirement.

> ✔ The staggered block layout (see Figure 3-2) is another way to show the fit between the employer's priorities and your assets.

The T-letter's mission

> ✔ To present a RedHot profile of you, perfectly matched to the employer's interests

> ✔ To pre-market your knowledge of the employer and the industry

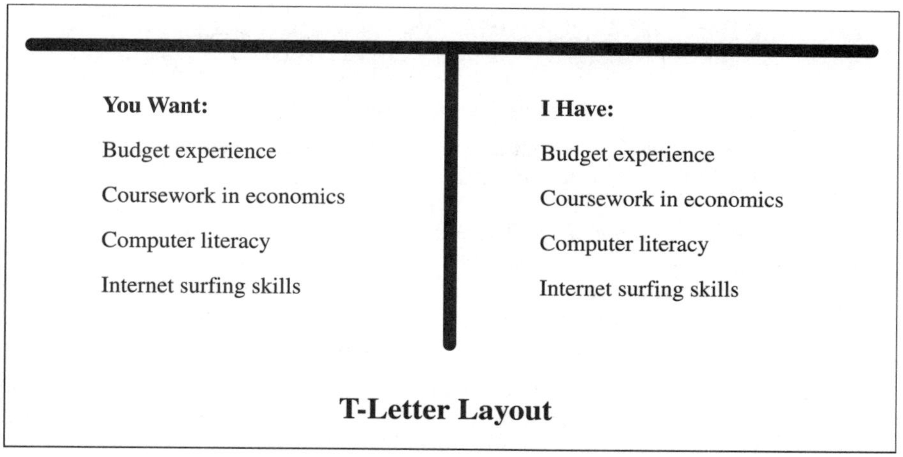

You Want:

Budget experience

Coursework in economics

Computer literacy

Internet surfing skills

I Have:

Budget experience

Coursework in economics

Computer literacy

Internet surfing skills

T-Letter Layout

Figure 3-1:
The ledger
layout is
the most
common
format for
the T-letter.

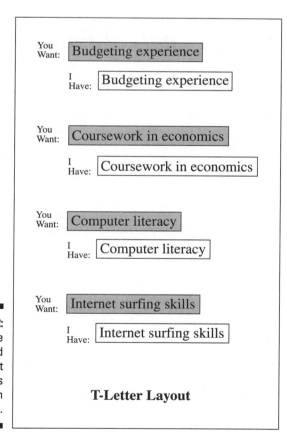

You
Want: Budgeting experience

I
Have: Budgeting experience

You
Want: Coursework in economics

I
Have: Coursework in economics

You
Want: Computer literacy

I
Have: Computer literacy

You
Want: Internet surfing skills

I
Have: Internet surfing skills

T-Letter Layout

Figure 3-2:
The
staggered
block layout
also works
well with
T-letters.

Advantages of the T-letter

- ✔ Instantly appeals to busy readers by performing the matching between job requirements and applicant qualifications
- ✔ Shows understanding of employer's priorities and limited time — shows that you're resourceful

Disadvantages of the T-letter

- ✔ Unsuitable if you're not a close match. Without RedHot spin control on areas of weakness, may show too many deficiencies of knowledge or absent credentials, experience, or education.
- ✔ Without employer research, knowledge of field, and rigorous self-assessment (see Chapters 5 and 6), the cross-matching may be too sparse to compete with other applicants.

The Blind Ad Letter: A Leap of Faith

The ideal cover letter addresses a single reader by name. However, many recruitment ads virtually prevent any form of targeting — unless you're a good detective (an issue discussed in my book, *Resumes For Dummies*). The advertisers provide only an untraceable fax number, P.O. box, commercial mail facility box, publication box, or cloaked e-mail address. They bypass the advertiser's name, job title, and department, leaving you clueless.

Once you have tried your hardest to ferret out the name and identity of your recipient, you may still be left with only a ghost employer.

Why do advertisers run blind ads? According to John D. Erdlen, president of Strategic Outsourcing Inc. (a division of ROMAC International), a leading human resource consulting group based in Wellesley, Massachusetts, employers place blind recruitment ads to

- ✔ Attract a surplus of responses without the complications of incoming telephone calls craftily bypassing clerical filters
- ✔ Maintain secrecy while exploring the market before deciding on an internal promotion or replacement
- ✔ Keep job openings secret from competitors who'd love to know where the hiring company has holes in its armor
- ✔ Avoid being overwhelmed with an avalanche of job seekers when they lack the staff to process all responses

The blind ad letter's mission

- ✔ To attract the reader's attention and spark active consideration of your candidacy for the position
- ✔ To respond to requirements listed in the ad with a competitive lineup of qualifications, skills, and results (drawn from your data developed in Chapters 5 and 6), and your knowledge of the industry plus a motivation to learn new skills

Advantages of the blind ad letter

- ✔ As many job seekers doubt the legitimacy of blind ads, considering them a waste of time, blind ads are often ignored — reducing your competition.
- ✔ Use it to show creativity and resourcefulness (especially if you can track down the name of the advertiser), which may bring surprising responses from those you were hoping to reach.

Disadvantages of the blind ad letter

- ✔ Without enough industry research, you risk missing the mystery reader's bullseye interests.
- ✔ Ghost recruitment ads can decrease the chances that your inquiry will be acknowledged, wasting your time; without an identity, you can't follow up.
- ✔ Without employer identity, the ad could be your current employer or one you have already contacted via some other avenue — rare, but possible.

Job hotline reply letter

You called a hotline; now what? Most job hotlines offer the name of an individual to call, or direct you to the employer's human resource department. In either case, your letter must address someone in particular, or your letter may be treated as junk mail.

Pay as much attention to job requirements given on the hotline as you would to a newspaper recruitment ad. The mission, advantages, and disadvantages are identical to those of other responding letters.

Usually you know the name of the company, but in a large organization, you may not be told the department or other particulars. When the hotline offers minimal information, dig around to find out more by calling the company's receptionist. If you're stonewalled by the receptionist or voice mail, follow the advice given for blind ad reply letters.

The Employment Service Letter

While shopping recruitment ads and online job postings, you may be asked to respond not to the employer but to the employer's third-party representative. You may be asked to contact

- ✔ Contract recruiters (specialists who fill short-term jobs, such as engineering contracts that last six months or longer) and temporary service consultants
- ✔ Executive recruiters and employment agencies
- ✔ Campus career center personnel

Be alert to wordings such as "client company," "our client," or similar expressions. This phrasing identifies the advertiser as an employment agency, executive recruiter, or other third-party employment service. Because these employment services represent an employer you hope to work for, address your letter to the employment service. If you know the name of the employer, you can state the employer's name in the RE: (Regarding) line or in the introduction to your letter.

Like most employers, employment services prefer letters that get to the point — preferably in less than one page. As with other RedHot cover letters, front-load your letter with your most marketable skills and experience (based on research for your career field).

The Targeted Resume Letter: All in One

The targeted resume letter is a combination of the cover letter and resume. It is also called a tailored letter. This letter is thought to be more personal, and thus more appealing, than the cover-letter-plus-resume duo.

This type of letter is more effective when sent directly to hiring managers rather than to the human resources department. In content, the targeted resume letter is similar to the broadcast letter described in Chapter 4.

To satisfy RedHot standards, incorporate employer research, skills, and information from your worksheets to showcase the jalapeño results employers are hungry for.

The targeted resume letter's mission

- ✔ To condense the resume and separate letter into two pages of friendly yet professional conversation
- ✔ To sketch a quick summary of your qualifications for the position — just enough for the reader to want more, but not enough to get you screened out of consideration

Advantages of the targeted resume letter

- ✔ Because these letters are obviously time-consuming to prepare, recipient may feel a greater obligation to read it rather than the letter-resume package
- ✔ Provides a less rigid, spartan context for information that may be dulled on a formal resume; with RedHot handling, can be a pleasure to read

Disadvantages of the targeted resume letter

- ✔ Time consuming to write; without RedHot spice, the letter may not contain enough information to show you are qualified for the position; if your background is extensive, you may shortchange yourself.
- ✔ Targeted resume letters don't look like resumes and may be perceived by conservative employers as negatively unconventional, especially at managerial levels.

Close Your Letter with Freshness

Before moving on to action letters that initiate leads, one more thought about closing your responding letters:

Sincerely yours works fine. But how about a professional yet interesting closing, such as:

> *Enthusiastic about joining your team,*

> *I look forward to meeting with you,*

> *Thanks for your consideration,*

> *Vigorously,*

What other lines can you think of to put morning dew on your responding letter?

Chapter 4
Action Letters That Initiate Leads

In This Chapter

▶ Writing when you hope a job opening exists
▶ Meeting the five-member family of initiating letters
▶ Pleasing by saying thank-you

*T*he job letter family is easier to understand if you think of two main groups of members:

✔ Action letters that **respond** to needs

   Letters in this group are written when you know a job opening exists. These are *reactive letters*. You can read more about responding letters in Chapter 3.

✔ Action letters that **initiate** leads

   Letters in this group are written to inquire about a possible job opening. These are *proactive letters*.

   Also in this category are thank-you letters and other letters you initiate as a way to follow up on a possible job opening.

You've toiled in the vineyards of responding letters and now you wonder what else you can possibly do while you anxiously await call-backs and interviews.

Well, you can seize the initiative and campaign for jobs that don't surface in recruitment advertising — jobs found in what has come to be known as the *hidden job market*.

Job search guru Tom Jackson coined the term *hidden job market* in the mid-1960s, using it as a book title in the early 1970s. As noted, the term refers to job openings or potential job openings that for one reason or another are not made public. In many cases, these are prime positions that become known through industry networking. Many of these jobs are filled from within the company (leaving another vacancy) or filled by candidates known or recommended by someone known to the employer. These are the jobs to which your networking skills can lead.

You can track down those job leads and write letters to nail down those leads. Action letters that proactively initiate leads do heavy lifting in any RedHot job search.

This chapter introduces you to five basic action-initiating letter categories — each of which can open doors to employment (model initiating letters can be found in Chapter 12). They are

- **Networking letter** — used to open job options in the companies that you target and to ferret out more job leads from your contacts
- **Follow-up letter** — used to thank employers for interviews, to remind employers and contacts of your interaction with them, and to encourage hiring action
- **Broadcast letter** — used in mailing campaigns to potential employers and executive recruiters
- **Recommendation letter** — used as reinforcement of your qualifications (you draft the letter for reference's signature)
- **Endgame letter** — used to accept or reject job offers

The Networking Letter: Reaching Out

Networking means making connections with people whom you may not yet know but who may be helpful in your job search. As author Max Messmer says in *Job Hunting For Dummies*, networking is based on the principle of being carried into a situation on another person's coattails: "It is easier to get information and help from people who either know you or know someone who knows you than from people who have never heard of you."

You can write networking letters to

- Employers
- Family
- Friends
- Co-workers (former and current)
- Fellow members of professional organizations
- Fellow members of service, religious, civic, fraternal, and political organizations
- Alumni, campus career center specialists, professors, classmates

✔ Employees of other companies in your field

✔ Internet contacts

Some networking letters, using a mutual friend's coattails, make memorable connections with potential employers, asking them for a job or soliciting advice and ideas.

Other networking letters ask everyone but potential employers for job leads or referrals.

The networking letter's mission

Use a networking letter to help you accomplish a number of useful goals.

When addressed to someone who can give you a job, your networking letter can be used

✔ To gain a job or referral by making a personal connection and establishing rapport. When you telephone, you can truthfully say that the employer is expecting your call (your letter specifies when you'll call)

✔ To gain priority over nonconnected applicants

When addressed to someone who can help you find a job, your networking letter can be used

✔ To get a referral or recommendation

✔ To get information on a target employer

✔ To get general advice on your course of action

Advantages and disadvantages

A well-written networking letter

✔ Establishes a broader base of job options

✔ Gives you priority over applicants who apply cold turkey

✔ Shows employers your personal connection with their companies and reduces their screening efforts

---

Networking letters to potential employers

When writing networking letters, mention

✔ How you came to write the letter (note reference or other lead)

✔ How your education and background have prepared you for the field

✔ Knowledge about issues the employer faces without appearing to tell the employer the employer's business; add lots of "as you know" qualifiers

---

As with most things useful in your job search, networking letters have disadvantages as well.

✔ Writing networking letters requires time and resourcefulness.

✔ Even the greatest networking letter does not guarantee success in job leads.

✔ Without RedHot tact, you may be misinterpreted as presumptuous.

The Follow-Up Letters: Circling Back

Follow-up letters are sent after something has happened — agreement to grant a job interview, the job interview itself, or some other action that suggests you're being helped into the employment process.

The thank-you letter to employers

Even if employers are not swayed by your thank-you letter, sending one never hurts. Think of letter-writing as a muscle that needs exercise.

The thank-you letter's mission

Before the job interview, write a thank-you letter

✔ To confirm the interview time and place

✔ To thank the interviewer for the appointment

✔ To add a selling point to increase the interviewer's anticipation of meeting you.

After the job interview, write a thank-you letter

- ✔ To immediately remind the interviewer of you and make yet another good impression

- ✔ To add information or ideas not covered in the interview — perhaps ideas suggested during the interview itself

- ✔ To provide another reason for the interviewer to contact you about your candidacy

Advantages and disadvantages

When you write a thank-you letter

- ✔ You look well mannered, or at least aware enough to be an asset to the company.

- ✔ Unless you write a poor letter, a thank-you letter always leaves a positive impression. There are no disadvantages.

Writing is one sure way to expose the quality of your thinking. Any time you set word processor to paper, you risk making a poor impression if you don't think things through carefully. Stay aware of the importance of each word you choose. If your writing skills are not strong, ask a friend to review your letter before you send it off.

The follow-up letter for a favor

You understand the need to write thank-you letters to potential employers. But you also need to remember all the others who help your job cause. Here's what I mean:

Suppose that last week you struck up a conversation with a woman at your gym, who turns out to be the administrative assistant at a firm you'd love to work for. She told you about an entry-level opening in its newest department, and she advised you to send in a resume and a cover letter.

You're not certain if she processes resumes and cover letters, but she's your only straight slide into the firm. Still sticky in your gym clothes, you're in front of your computer, coping with writer's block and a blank screen. You need a job letter — a follow-up letter — to remind her of your meeting, and you need to send it within the next 24 hours! Write it!

The follow-up letter is a close relative of the networking letter. Both cement a continuing relationship between networking contacts and employers with whom you have not yet interviewed.

The follow-up letter's mission

Use a follow-up letter

- ✔ To remind the contact of your connection
- ✔ To follow up when an employer (as a result of a contact or networking letter) invites you to send your resume
- ✔ To encourage contacts to forward your resume to employers
- ✔ To establish continued rapport in case an opening should arise in the future

Advantages and disadvantages of a follow-up letter

A follow-up letter

- ✔ Personally connects you to employer inroads
- ✔ Communicates an interested brand of aggressiveness and enthusiasm about the opening
- ✔ Provides the contact with a permanent reminder of a promise to help you

The downside of a follow-up letter, as with any writing effort, is that

- ✔ You may need to write a number of these before one produces a solid lead or interview.
- ✔ You may need several time-consuming attempts before you compose and effective letter.

The Broadcast Letter: Giant Mailings

You may have heard of the broadcast letter, otherwise known as the "direct mail campaign resume letter." You may even have decided that this approach is your best bet for broadest job coverage.

The broadcast letter combines a resume with a cover letter. Advocates of broadcast letters say that the technique works when you invest in big numbers (like one or two thousand letters). The numbers shrink when you mail to executive recruiters (as noted in Chapter 14, sending to a select list of a few hundred executive recruiters is recommended as a good way to jump start a job search).

Detractors say the mass outreach of broadcast letters is a waste of time and money.

I've never seen a study scientifically proving whether broadcast letters work or not. If you try the technique, take care in selecting your mailing list and write one wowser of a letter.

The broadcast letter's mission

Use a broadcast letter

- ✔ To replace the resume
- ✔ To present your qualifications quickly to a hiring manager with the power to hire you (not human resource department personnel)
- ✔ To publicize your availability to employers in a hard-hitting, self-marketing format

Advantages and disadvantages of the broadcast letter

The broadcast letter has a number of advantages. It

- ✔ Combines resume and cover letter into one compact seller
- ✔ Includes pertinent information from your resume not usually found in other cover letters
- ✔ With RedHot sell, may save recruiters time and money in their searches
- ✔ Gets more attention than most junk mail

The disadvantages of the broadcast letter are that it

- ✔ Relies on getting the reader's attention in the first couple of seconds
- ✔ May appear lazy or vague without careful assessment of background
- ✔ Is time consuming, and you may receive few or no responses

The broadcast letter is a favorite technique of outplacement firms and some cover letter readers may consider it overplayed.

If your broadcast letter does not address specific individuals, or if it addresses the wrong individuals, you may as well feed it to the neighborhood goat.

The Recommendation Letter: Getting Endorsements

The employer you've been hopping around on pins and needles waiting to hear from just left a message on your e-mail asking for several letters of recommendation.

Don't panic — write your own recommendations! Remembering that just about everyone in the working world is as busy as (if not busier than) you, contact individuals in a position to recommend you (such as previous employers, professors, and leaders of organizations or clubs).

If your references are willing to sing your praises, offer to draft a letter for their fine-tuning.

For your references' convenience and your peace of mind, find out what word processing program they use. Draft the letter(s) on that program and save them on floppy disks. Hand deliver or mail your references both a disk and a printed copy.

Alternatively, e-mail is a great way to forward the draft of your recommendation letter, but doing so may slightly affect your graphic presentation. If your reference subscribes to the same online commercial service as you (such as America Online, or CompuServe), the graphics will not be affected.

The Endgame Letter: Wrapping Up

You're well into your job search. Maybe your search has stalled out and you need to restart it. Or perhaps you've been offered a job. You still have letters to write.

- ✔ Resurrection letters
- ✔ Acceptance letters
- ✔ Rejection letters

The *resurrection letter's* mission is to remind an employer of your application (perhaps they stalled their recruitment) or to revive your application after having removed yourself from consideration. In short order, remind the reader of

- ✔ Your last communication with the employer
- ✔ A positive narrative of what has happened since that time
- ✔ Your top selling points for the position (include another copy of your resume)
- ✔ A statement of your continued interest in the position and the company's search

The difference between fizzle and sizzle

In drafting your recommendation letter for another's signature, bear these thoughts in mind:

- Identify your reference — who the person is, what the person does, and where the person does it.

- Give a clear statement of who is being recommended (you) and for what position.

- Add a narrative of the reference's relationship to you — how long, in what capacity, how closely, and what projects were shared.

- Include a time when the reference can be contacted for more information.

- Provide a flash-list of your top skills, judgment, work habits, reliability, productivity, compatibility, field knowledge, attributes, and achievements, as well as how these qualities benefit the prospective position.

- If your references prefer to write their own letters, review with them the above points in case they have fewer, less RedHot details in mind. Take no chances. A wishy-washy recommendation can cool your candidacy.

The *acceptance letter's* mission is not only to thank the hiring party, but also to define the terms of your employment as agreed upon in your interview/job offer negotiations. Such terms include

- Salary
- Job title
- Benefits
- Contract terms

While this letter may seem like overkill, it's actually a cover-your-butt letter — your terms are in writing in case anything goes awry. Send one to each individual directly involved in your recruitment.

The *rejection* letter also covers your butt; if you don't answer other employers' job offers, you may create enemies.

- Courteously thank employers for their time, interviews, and consideration.

- Inform them that you have already accepted another offer (you may not wish to say from whom) and are no longer available.

- Include any hopes you may have to work with them in the future.

Whether making friends or covering your butt, these EndGame letters finalize the employment end of your job hunt.

RedHot phrases for acceptance letters

"I am delighted to accept your generous offer to become your company's (job title)."

"I appreciate the confidence you demonstrated by selecting me to be (job title)."

"This letter is my acceptance of your offer to join (name of company) as (job title)."

"I look forward to becoming a part of your team as (job title), beginning (start date)."

"I eagerly anticipate the challenges in the position as (job title) that you have offered me."

"I would like to express my gratitude in accepting the position of (job title); I look forward to the challenges and responsibilities that the position offers."

Part II
Working Out What Sizzles

The 5th Wave   By Rich Tennant

"No, I don't think including a lock of your hair is the right way to personalize your cover letter."

In this part . . .

You wouldn't attempt to enter yourself in Olympic competition without extensive preparation. For that matter, you probably wouldn't enter a 6K walk without at least trying to condition your body. And you spent a great deal of time acquiring the skills for the career you want. So what makes you think that you can write cover letters without stretching some intellectual muscle?

Truthfully, you know that cover letters require time and concentration, or you wouldn't be reading this book. This part lets you exercise your skill-finding tendons with worksheets and up-to-date skill listings so that you can run and, more importantly, win your own race for a good job.

Chapter 5

JobSeeker's Skills Finder

. . . .

. . . .

*T*he next big buzzword on the job search horizon is *skills*. A related buzzword is *skills certification*.

Haven't skills always been a centerpiece in the hiring arrangement? Yes, they have. But their degree of importance is going up like a rocket. Within the next few years, I predict that the concept of skills will explode in the marketplace. Books about skills will be written; seminars teaching skill identification will flourish; and trainers will clue supervisors about techniques to recognize skills in employees.

The reason for this emphasis on skills is that we're living through an evolving and unpredictable job market where skills that applicants bring to the job eclipse every other factor in hiring.

Small businesses are creating most of the new jobs, and small companies have fewer resources to use in training new hires. So the skills for which you don't need to be trained are paramount. Moreover, large companies are racked by advancing technology that makes jobs obsolete or surplus, and by management decisions that dispose of workers to boost returns for investors.The more skills you have, the more likely you are to be retained when corporate downsizing starts its slide.

Corporate America used to have a hiring policy of *hire-until-retire*. This policy has been replaced by *hire-until-fire*, as illustrated by this paraphrasing of a statement recently issued to employees by a U.S. corporate giant:

> *Don't expect to spend a lifetime with us. You'll be here 5, 10 — perhaps 15 years. Take responsibility for your career. Don't count on us as corporate parents.*

Many job tenures are downgraded in this new sunset hiring style where jobs are destined to be phased out in two to three years — or, for contract jobs, even 6 to 18 months.

All these changes add up to an increased demand for people who can hit the floor running — people who require little on-job training to become immediately productive. The only people who fit these new and demanding criteria are people with specific, marketable skills.

You can prove your skills by *demonstration* (you show), *inference* (your prior education and experience show), *assertion* (you claim), *references* (others claim on your behalf), and *certification* (you prove skills by testing and peer evaluation).

If you are to master the competition in the new workplaces of America, follow these rules:

1. **Be ready to identify your skills and to explain how your skills make you immediately productive to a new employer.**

2. **If you do not have marketable skills, get some by whatever means available to you, from on-job training to formal education.**

3. **Follow rule number 1 — again and again.**

Where There's a Skill There's a Way

Analyzing skills only looks easy. The task can prove challenging even when you know what you're doing. A practical way to organize skills for job-seeking purposes is to divide them into three basic types: transferable skills, employability skills, and technical skills.

✔ **Transferable skills:** Transferable skills are your most important skills — portable skills that you can use in job after job. They answer an employer's question: *"Can* you do the job?" Because they apply to a variety of jobs, they can be considered *nonspecific.* For example, employers value communications skills in jobs ranging from apple grower to zoo keeper. You can transfer these skills from job to job, or even from one career field to another career field.

✔ **Employability skills:** Employability skills are personal skills that answer the employer's questions: *"Will* you do the job? *Will* you do the job in harmony with other employees? Also called *adaptive* or *self-management skills*, these skills can be considered *person-specific.* For example, reliability, honesty, enthusiasm, and getting along with others illustrate characteristics included in employability skills. Employability skills suggest character and attitudes — who you are and how you work.

✔ **Technical skills:** Technical skills are job-related skills, suitable for a particular type of job. They also answer an employer's question, *"Can* you do the job?" Often you can't easily move technical skills from one employer to another, and so these skills are considered *job-specific.* For example, the ability to use a certain brand of mold-injection machine classifies as a technical skill.

Here's a common-sense tip: Mention your technical skill(s) only when you are certain that a prospective employer can benefit from the technical skill(s) you bring. Unless you are positive the employer can use your technical skill(s), stick to transferable skills in your cover letter and resume.

Discovering Your Skills

Because the skills concept is becoming such a hot issue, I give you a couple of checklists to help you roundup and brand those you own. Don't get creative and adopt a skill just because it looks good on paper or when you're not sure what the word means. If you don't know what a word or a term means, look it up or don't use it. You can expect to be grilled on your skill claims during a job interview. Prepare to support each skill claim with quantifiable evidence.

Read through these transferable and employability skills checklists and mark those words and terms that apply to you. Include those terms as part of your skills language to take with you from job to job.

I don't include a technical skills checklist because those skills vary according to each individual's job area.

Skills: Your count or mine?

It's a matter of opinion how skills are classified. Some advisers, for instance, divide skills into only two categories: work content and functional.

Work-content skills are used to perform a specific type of job, such as financial planning or computer programming; they are learned through school or work experience.

Functional skills are transferable, learned across careers, jobs, and industries.

The classification scheme isn't important. What counts in a job search is being able to sell yourself by identifying your skills.

Transferable Skills Checklist

A

❏ Accelerating

❏ Accomplishing

❏ Accounting

❏ Accuracy

❏ Achieving

❏ Activating

❏ Active

❏ Active learning

❏ Active listening

❏ Adapting

❏ Addressing

❏ Adjusting

❏ Administering

❏ Advertising

❏ Advising

❏ Aiding

❏ Allocating

❏ Altering

❏ Amending

❏ Analyzing behavior

❏ Analyzing costs

❏ Announcing

❏ Anticipating

❏ Appearance

❏ Application

❏ Appointing

❏ Appraising

❏ Appreciation

❏ Arbitrating

❏ Argumentation

❏ Arranging

❏ Articulation

❏ Assembling

❏ Assessing cost

❏ Assessing damage

❏ Assigning

❏ Assisting

❏ Attaining

❏ Attending

❏ Auditing

❏ Augmenting

❏ Authoring

❏ Automating

B

❏ Balancing

❏ Bargaining

❏ Blending

❏ Bookkeeping

❏ Boosting

❏ Bridging

❏ Briefing

❏ Budgeting

❏ Building

C

❏ Calculating

❏ Calibrating

❏ Cataloging

❏ Categorizing

❏ Chairing

❏ Charting

❏ Checking

❏ Clarifying

❏ Classifying

❏ Clerical ability

❏ Coaching

❏ Coaxing

❏ Cognizance

❏ Coherence

❏ Collaborative

❏ Combining

❏ Comforting

❏ Commanding

❏ Communicating

❏ Comparing

❏ Competence

❏ Compiling

❏ Complimenting

❏ Composing

❏ Compromising

❏ Computing

❏ Condensing

❏ Conducting

❏ Confidentiality

❏ Conflict resolution

❏ Conforming

❏ Confronting

❏ Consolidating

❏ Constructing

❏ Consulting

❏ Contingency planning

❏ Contracting

❏ Controlling

❏ Converting

❏ Convincing

❏ Cooperation

❏ Coordinating

❏ Copying

❏ Correcting

❏ Correlating

❏ Corresponding

❏ Counseling

❏ Counteracting

❏ Counterbalancing

❏ Counting

❏ Creating

❏ Creative writing

❏ Crisis management

D

❏ Data collecting

❏ Data entry

❏ Debating

❏ Decision making

❏ Deductive reasoning

❏ Defending

❏ Defining problems

❏ Delegating

❏ Delivering

❏ Demonstrating

- ❏ Depicting
- ❏ Describing
- ❏ Designating
- ❏ Designing
- ❏ Detecting
- ❏ Developing ideas
- ❏ Devising
- ❏ Diagnosing
- ❏ Diagramming
- ❏ Diplomacy
- ❏ Directing
- ❏ Discretion
- ❏ Discussing
- ❏ Dispatching
- ❏ Dispensing
- ❏ Displaying
- ❏ Distributing
- ❏ Diversifying
- ❏ Diverting
- ❏ Documenting
- ❏ Drafting
- ❏ Drawing
- ❏ Duplicating

E

- ❏ Editing
- ❏ Educating

- ❏ Effecting change
- ❏ Elevating
- ❏ Eliminating
- ❏ Empowering
- ❏ Enabling
- ❏ Enacting
- ❏ Encouraging
- ❏ Engineering a plan
- ❏ Enhancing
- ❏ Enlarging
- ❏ Enlisting
- ❏ Enlivening
- ❏ Enriching
- ❏ Envisioning
- ❏ Equalizing
- ❏ Escalating
- ❏ Establishing objectives
- ❏ Establishing priorities
- ❏ Estimating
- ❏ Evaluating
- ❏ Examining
- ❏ Exchanging information
- ❏ Executing a plan
- ❏ Exhibiting
- ❏ Expanding
- ❏ Expediting
- ❏ Extracting

F

- ❏ Fabricating
- ❏ Facilitating
- ❏ Figuring
- ❏ Filing
- ❏ Finding
- ❏ Finishing
- ❏ Fixing
- ❏ Fluency
- ❏ Following through
- ❏ Forecasting
- ❏ Foresight
- ❏ Forging
- ❏ Forming
- ❏ Formulating
- ❏ Fostering
- ❏ Founding
- ❏ Framing
- ❏ Fulfilling
- ❏ Fundraising
- ❏ Furthering

G

- ❏ Gauging
- ❏ Generalizing
- ❏ Generating
- ❏ Grammar

❑ Graphics

❑ Grouping

❑ Guessing

❑ Guiding

H

❑ Handling complaints

❑ Harmonizing

❑ Heading

❑ Healing

❑ Helpful

❑ Hypothesizing

I

❑ Identifying alternatives

❑ Identifying causes

❑ Identifying downstream consequences

❑ Identifying issues

❑ Identifying needs

❑ Identifying principles

❑ Identifying problems

❑ Illuminating

❑ Illustrating

❑ Impartial

❑ Implementing

❑ Improving

❑ Incitement

❑ Increasing

❑ Indexing

❑ Indoctrinating

❑ Inducive

❑ Inductive reasoning

❑ Influencing

❑ Information gathering

❑ Information management

❑ Information organization

❑ Information receiving

❑ Informing

❑ Infusing

❑ Insightful

❑ Inspecting

❑ Inspiring

❑ Installation

❑ Instilling

❑ Instituting

❑ Instruction

❑ ntegration

❑ Interaction

❑ Interceding

❑ Interpersonal skills

❑ Interpretation

❑ Interrupting

❑ Intervening

❑ Interviewing

❑ Introducing

❑ Investigation

❑ Isolating

❑ Itemizing

J

❑ Joining

❑ Judgment

K

❑ Keeping deadlines

❑ Keyboarding

❑ Knowledge of subject

L

❑ Language

❑ Launching

❑ Laying

❑ Leadership

❑ Learning

❑ Lecturing

❑ Listening for content

❑ Listening for context

❑ Listening for directions

❑ Listening for emotional meaning

❑ Listing

❑ Locating

❏ Logical reasoning

❏ Long-term planning

M

❏ Maintaining confidentiality

❏ Maintenance

❏ Managing

❏ Maneuvering

❏ Manipulation

❏ Mapping

❏ Marketing

❏ Masking

❏ Matching

❏ Mathematics

❏ Measuring

❏ Mechanical ability

❏ Mediating

❏ Meeting

❏ Mending

❏ Mentoring

❏ Merchandising

❏ Minding machines

❏ Minimizing

❏ Modeling

❏ Moderating

❏ Modifying

❏ Modulating

❏ Molding

❏ Money management

❏ Monitoring

❏ Motivating

N

❏ Negotiating

❏ Nonpartisan

❏ Number skills

❏ Nursing

❏ Nurturing

O

❏ Objectivity

❏ Observing

❏ Operating vehicles

❏ Operations analysis

❏ Oral communication

❏ Oral comprehension

❏ Orchestrating

❏ Organizational effectiveness

❏ Organizing

❏ Outfitting

❏ Outlining

❏ Outreach

❏ Overhauling

❏ Overseeing

P

❏ Pacifying

❏ Paraphrasing

❏ Participating

❏ Patterning

❏ Perceiving

❏ Perfecting

❏ Performing

❏ Persuasion

❏ Photography

❏ Picturing

❏ Pinpointing

❏ Planning

❏ Plotting

❏ Policy making

❏ Polishing

❏ Politicking

❏ Popularizing

❏ Portraying

❏ Precision

❏ Prediction

❏ Preparation

❏ Presentation

❏ Printing

❏ Prioritizing

❏ Probing

❏ Problem-solving

❏ Processing

❏ Producing

❏ Professional

❏ Prognostication

❏ Program design

❏ Program developing

❏ Program implementation

❏ Projection

❏ Promoting

❏ Proofreading

❏ Proposing

❏ Protecting

❏ Providing

❏ Public speaking

❏ Publicizing

❏ Publishing

❏ Purchasing

Q

❏ Quality control

R

❏ Raising

❏ Ranking

❏ Readiness

❏ Reading comprehension

❏ Reasoning

❏ Reclaiming

❏ Recognition

❏ Reconciling

❏ Recording

❏ Recovering

❏ Recruiting

❏ Rectifying

❏ Reducing

❏ Referring

❏ Reformative

❏ Regulating

❏ Rehabilitating

❏ Reinforcing

❏ Relationship building

❏ Remodeling

❏ Rendering

❏ Reorganizing

❏ Repairing

❏ Repeating

❏ Reporting

❏ Representing

❏ Researching

❏ Resolving

❏ Resource development

❏ Resource management

❏ Response coordination

❏ Restoring

❏ Restructuring

❏ Retrieving

❏ Reversing

❏ Reviewing

❏ Revitalizing

❏ Rhetoric

❏ Rousing

❏ Running

S

❏ Saving

❏ Scanning

❏ Scheduling

❏ Schooling

❏ Science

❏ Scientific reasoning

❏ Screening

❏ Scrutiny

❏ Searching

❏ Selecting

❏ Selling

❏ Sensitivity

❏ Sequencing

❏ Serving

❏ Setting up

❏ Settling

❏ Shaping

❏ Shielding

❏ Situation analysis

❏ Sketching

❏ Social perceptiveness

❏ Solidifying

❏ Solution appraisal

❏ Solving

❏ Sorting

❏ Speaking

❏ Spearheading

❏ Specialization

❏ Specifying

❏ Speculating

❏ Speech

❏ Stabilizing

❏ Stimulating

❏ Stirring

❏ Storing information

❏ Streamlining

❏ Strengthening

❏ Structuring

❏ Styling

❏ Substituting

❏ Summarizing

❏ Supervising

❏ Supplementing

❏ Supporting

❏ Surmising

❏ Surveying

❏ Sustaining

❏ Synthesis

❏ Systematizing

❏ Systems analysis

❏ Systems management

❏ Systems perception

❏ Systems understanding

T

❏ Tabulating

❏ Taking instruction

❏ Talking

❏ Teaching

❏ Teamwork

❏ Technical writing

❏ Tempering

❏ Terminology

❏ Testing

❏ Theorizing

❏ Time management

❏ Training

❏ Translating

❏ Traveling

❏ Treating

❏ Troubleshooting

❏ Tutoring

❏ Typing

U

❏ Unifying

❏ Updating

❏ Upgrading

❏ Using tools

V

❏ Values clarification

❏ Visual communication

W

❏ Word processing

❏ Working with earth

❏ Working with nature

❏ Working with others

❏ Written communication

Your top transferable skills

Select your top six transferable skills from those you marked in this chapter. Keep these top transferable skills in mind as you look for validation of each one while doing the worksheets in Chapter 6. (You'll also unearth additional transferable skills in working your Chapter 6 worksheets.)

1. _____

2. _____

3. _____

4. _____

5. _____

6. _____

Employability Skills Checklist

A

❏ Ability to learn

❏ Abstract thinking

❏ Accepting onsequences

❏ Ability to learn

❏ Abstract thinking

❏ Accepting consequences

❏ Accepting criticism

❏ Accepting freedom

❏ Accepting supervision

❏ Accommodating

❏ Active

❏ Adventurous

❏ Affable

❏ Agile

❏ Alert

❏ Ambitious

❏ Amicable

❏ Animated

❏ Appealing

❏ Approachable

❏ Artistic abilities

❏ Aspiring

❏ Assertive

❏ Astute

❏ Athletic

❏ Attendance

❏ Attention to detail

❏ Autonomy

❏ Awareness

B

❑ Benevolent

❑ Benign

❑ Bold

❑ Brave

❑ Bright

C

❑ Careful

❑ Caring

❑ Casual

❑ Cautious

❑ Charismatic

❑ Charitable

❑ Charming

❑ Cheerful

❑ Chivalrous

❑ Clever

❑ Colorful

❑ Commitment

❑ Common sense

❑ Compassion

❑ Compliant

❑ Composure

❑ Comprehension

❑ Concentration

❑ Conceptualization

❑ Concern

❑ Confidence

❑ Congenial

❑ Conscientious

❑ Conservative

❑ Considerate

❑ Consistent

❑ Constant

❑ Contemplative

❑ Cordial

❑ Courageous

❑ Courteous

❑ Creativity

❑ Critical thinking

❑ Cunning

❑ Curiosity

D

❑ Daring

❑ Decisive

❑ Dedicated

❑ Deft

❑ Deliberate

❑ Dependable

❑ Desire

❑ Determined

❑ Devoted

❑ Devout

❑ Dexterity

❑ Dignity

❑ Diligent

❑ Discipline

❑ Dogged

❑ Drive

❑ Dutiful

❑ Dynamic

E

❑ Eager

❑ Earnest

❑ Easy-going

❑ Economical

❑ Efficient

❑ Eloquence

❑ Empathy

❑ Energetic

❑ Engaging

❑ Enjoys challenge

❑ Enterprising

❑ Entertaining

❑ Enthusiasm

❑ Entrepreneurial

❑ Ethical

❑ Exciting

❏ Explorative

❏ Expression

❏ Extemporizing

❏ Extroverted

F

❏ Fair

❏ Faithful

❏ Fast

❏ Firm

❏ Flexibility

❏ Focused

❏ Forceful

❏ Fortitude

❏ Friendly

❏ Funny

G

❏ Generous

❏ Gentle

❏ Genuine

❏ Gifted

❏ Good-natured

❏ Graceful

❏ Gracious

H

❏ Hardworking

❏ Hardy

❏ Honest

❏ Honor

❏ Humble

❏ Humorous

❏ Hustle

I

❏ Imagination

❏ Immaculate

❏ Impetus

❏ Improvisation

❏ Incentive

❏ Independent

❏ Industrious

❏ Informal

❏ Ingenious

❏ Initiative

❏ Innovative

❏ Inquisitive

❏ Integrity

❏ Intelligence

❏ Interest

❏ Intuitive

❏ Inventing

K

❏ Keen

❏ Kind

L

❏ Likable

❏ Lively

❏ Loyal

M

❏ Maturity

❏ Memory

❏ Methodical

❏ Meticulous

❏ Mindful

❏ Modest

❏ Motivation

N

❏ Neat

❏ Nimble

O

❏ Obliging

❏ Open-minded

❏ Opportunistic

❏ Optimistic

❏ Orderly

❏ Original

❏ Outgoing

P

❏ Painstaking

❏ Patience

❏ Perfectionist

❏ Persevering

❏ Persistence

❏ Personable

❏ Pioneering

❏ Pleasant

❏ Poised

❏ Polite

❏ Positive

❏ Powerful

❏ Practical

❏ Pragmatic

❏ Presence

❏ Pride

❏ Progressive

❏ Prompt

❏ Prudent

❏ Punctuality

Q

❏ Questioning

❏ Quick-thinking

R

❏ Rational

❏ Realistic

❏ Reasonable

❏ Receptive

❏ Reflective

❏ Relentless

❏ Reliable

❏ Reserved

❏ Resolute

❏ Respectful

❏ Responsible

❏ Responsiveness

❏ Restraint

❏ Retention

❏ Reverent

❏ Risk taking

❏ Robust

S

❏ Safety

❏ Savvy

❏ Scrupulous

❏ Self-esteem

❏ Self-motivating

❏ Self-reliant

❏ Self-respect

❏ Sense of humor

❏ Sensible

❏ Sharp

❏ Showmanship

❏ Shrewd

❏ Sincere

❏ Smart

❏ Sociable

❏ Spirited

❏ Stalwart

❏ Stamina

❏ Staunch

❏ Steadfast

❏ Steady

❏ Striving

❏ Strong

❏ Studious

❏ Sturdy

❏ Style

T

❏ Tactful

❏ Tasteful

❏ Tenacious

❏ Thinking

❏ Thorough

❏ Thoughtfulness

❏ Trustworthy

U

❏ Unbiased

❏ Understanding

❏ Unprejudiced

❏ Unpretentious

❏ Unselfish

V

❏ Venturing

❏ Versatile

❏ Vigilant

❏ Vigorous

❏ Visualizing

❏ Vivacious

W

❏ Warm

❏ Wary

❏ Watchful

❏ Willingness to follow rules

❏ Wisdom

❏ Work ethic

❏ Work habits

❏ Working alone

❏ Working under pressure

Your top employability skills

Select your top six employability skills from those you marked in this chapter. Keep these top employability skills in mind as you look for validation of each one while doing the worksheets in Chapter 6. (You'll also unearth additional employability skills in working with your Chapter 6 worksheets.)

1. _____

2. _____

3. _____

4. _____

5. _____

6. _____

Basic Skills Employers Want

You know the skills *you* have to offer, but how do you know which of those skills *to* offer? According to a study by the American Society for Training and Development and the U.S. Department of Labor, reading, writing, and arithmetic are no longer enough for a perfect job candidate. Based on the study, here's the hot gossip on employers' favorite skills.

The main skills employers want fall into four categories:

- ✔ **Effective communication:** Employers seek candidates who can listen to instructions and act on those instructions with minimal guidance. They want employees who speak and write effectively, organizing their thoughts logically and explaining everything clearly.

- ✔ **Problem-solving:** Problem-solving ability can aid you with transactions, data processing, formulating a vision, and reaching a resolution. Employers need the assurance that you can conquer job challenges.

- ✔ **Organization:** Life in the working world requires prioritizing and organizing information. The tidier your mental file-folders, the clearer your focus.

- ✔ **Leadership:** Leadership consists of a strong sense of self, confidence, and comprehensive knowledge of company goals. These are qualities that motivate and inspire, providing a solid foundation for teamwork.

Grammar grill: Watch the tense

The checklists I provide contain nouns and adjectives as well as verbs, which are usually expressed as gerunds (words ending in *-ing*). Watch the verbs: they hold the potential for ambush. Here's what I mean:

Saying that you are employed from "19XX to Present" suggests that you are still working. Use the present tense of verbs for current activities.

Some people, who really are working, forget about this and use the past tense of verbs. That error invites the employer to think: "She is trying to put one over on me. This applicant is really out of a job, but wants me to think that she is currently employed."

If you have the skills and are using them now in your job, use the present tense.

Employers' HotSkills buzzwords

1. Listening

2. Communicating clearly

3. Problem-solving

4. Showing leadership

5. Goal-setting/achieving

6. Self-motivating

7. Showing confidence

8. Organizing

9. Conceptualizing

10. Negotiating

The New Job Insurance: Certification

More than 43 million jobs have been erased in the United States since 1979, according to a *New York Times* analysis of U.S. Labor Department numbers. In an ongoing game of musical jobs, long-lasting employment has slipped into the shadows for people everywhere.

What help is there to make your skills portable, to carry you along the waves of opportunity? One answer is *credentialing,* or *certification.*

The nuts and bolts of certification

A professional certification can be a kind of passport, identifying you as a citizen of a career field with all its rank and privilege. In other words, professional credentialing is one way to document your ownership of the skills you claim.

Not all credentials are worthy. A credential is worth the effort it takes to get it only if it has industry recognition and respect. Even so, given the circumstances, certification is almost sure to become a growth industry before the century ends.

Here's a crash course on certification.

Differences in certification exist, but for ease of communication, I include other terms of validation such as *registered, accredited, chartered, qualified,* and *diplomate,* as well as *certified.* Whether the professional designation carries statutory clout or is voluntary, common elements include professional experience, often between two and ten years, sometimes reduced by education. Education standards are included, which may call for minimum levels of both academic and professional education.

Certification examinations, which may be one or several, are uninviting to many professionals — generally, they require time-consuming study and may include both experience-based knowledge acquired working in the field, and curriculum-based knowledge gained by assigned learning texts.

Membership in the certification-granting organization may be required, as well as professional recommendations. Rarely does certification come cheap. Costs can run from a few hundred to a few thousand dollars.

What's certification worth?

Is certification worth your effort?

Certification has strong appeal in your early career — say, the first 12 to 15 years — as a technique to control your earnings environment. But, in business, certifications lose their luster at the vice-presidential level and above. Why? Certifications zero in on specific skills, while top managers are more concerned with the big picture. For consulting, medicine, law, and technology careers, professional certifications never lose their punch, especially for those who hope to work internationally.

The credential may be a license awarded by a state board, such as the familiar certified public accountant (CPA), or a voluntary program sponsored by a professional organization, such as the designation of accredited in public relations (APR) awarded by the Public Relations Society of America.

Because a given professional certification may not carry stripes for your sleeve, much less stars for your shoulder, investigate first. Clues to look for include the following: Do recruitment ads call for the professional designation? Do trade journals mention it? What do practitioners in your field advise?

✔ As you change jobs more often, certification can be a kind of passport. It shows that you're a player in your field's global body of knowledge and that you have documented standards and achievements.

✔ Certification can be very helpful if you become sidetracked into too narrow a specialty or stagnate in a company with antiquated technologies or find yourself boxed in by a hostile boss. The boss can still claim you lack interpersonal abilities, but a professional designation leaves little room to say you're short on technical skills.

> ✔ You may earn more money going the certified route. A study of management accountants showed those holding the certified management accountant (CMA) designation outearn those who do not by about $9,000 to $15,000 yearly.

Need more? Check your library for a standard reference: *Guide to National Professional Certification Programs* by Phillip Barnhart (HRD Press). It details more than 500 certification programs, indexed by occupation.

No Frills, Just Skills

Now that you can speak a few words in skills talk, turn to the worksheets in Chapter 6. You'll review your education, jobs, and other experiences to find examples of the skills you claim — and you'll look for other skills you may have overlooked. By now you know that all this fuss over skills is because **Skills Sell!**

Chapter 6

Worksheets: Sorting Out Your Qualifications

In This Chapter

▶ Identifying your strengths and the facts that support them

▶ Discovering the positive differences you can make

*B*efore you can write a RedHot cover letter, you need raw materials to spotlight the RedHot features that interest potential buyers. The following worksheets identify your most marketable features; they also encourage you to translate those features into benefits for your target employer.

Worksheets are strength builders because filling them out helps you recall all the good things you have done. For instance, in reviewing your last job, think about these issues:

✔ What did you do?

✔ What did you direct others to do?

✔ What did you manage, create, approve, or instigate?

✔ What was the outcome of your actions?

　　　— More profits? (How much?)
　　　— More revenue? (How much?)
　　　— More accounts (How many? What are they worth?)

Every holiday season, *It's a Wonderful Life*, the classic Frank Capra film, is brought out of storage, dusted off, and shown again. Millions of viewers each year discover the story of the small town banker, George Bailey, who decides not to end his life after an angel helps him see what would have happened to the townspeople had Bailey not been on the job. He made a difference.

By now you know that the heyday of hiring is over — and you must take responsibility for the welfare of your career. Define your skills and what you bring to a new job. Consider what would have happened to others affected by your performance in your last position had you not been there.

After you finish the main worksheets, use the four summary exercises to reinforce the concept that you make a difference.

Education and Training Worksheet

(Photocopy and fill out one worksheet for each experience.)

Name of institution/program _____

Address/telephone _____

_____

_____

Year(s) _____ Degree/diploma/certificate _____

Overall GPA ____ Major GPA ___ Class rank (if known) _____

Work-relevant course and grade received _____

_____

_____

_____

_____

Knowledge acquired _____

Skills acquired _____

Accomplishments/Experience (with concrete examples) _____

_____

Relevant projects/papers/honors _____

Merit scholarships _____

Quotable remarks by others (names/contact data) _____

_____

How does education/training relate to the objective of the letter? _____

_____

Paid Work Worksheet

(Photocopy and fill out one or more worksheets for each job you've had.)

Employer's name (postal address, e-mail address, telephone, fax) _____

_____

_____

_____

Type of business/career field _____

Job title _____

Dates _____

Direct supervisor's name, contact information (use this person's name if a good reference; otherwise note co-workers or sources of good references)

_____

Major accomplishments (Promotion? Awards? Business achievements — "increased sales by 30 percent" or "saved company 12 percent on office pur-chases." What credit can you claim for creating, implementing, revamping, designing, or saving? Jog your memory by recalling problems faced and action taken.)

Problem faced _____

Action taken _____

Skills acquired _____

_____

Job responsibilities _____

Quotable remarks by others (names, contact data) _____

_____

_____

_____

Relate paid work to the objective of the letter _____

_____

_____

Unpaid Work Worksheet

(Photocopy and fill out one or more worksheets for each organization.)

Volunteer organization site (postal address, e-mail address, telephone, fax)

_____

_____

_____

Type of organization _____

Volunteer job title _____

Dates _____

Direct supervisor's name, contact information _____

_____

Major accomplishments (What credit can you claim for creating, implementing, revamping, designing, or saving? Jog your memory by recalling problems faced and action taken.)

   Problem faced _____

   Action taken _____

Skills acquired _____

_____

Job responsibilities _____

_____

Quotable remarks by others (names, contact data) _____

_____

_____

_____

Relate unpaid work to the objective of the letter _____

_____

Hobbies/Activities-to-Skills Worksheet

(Photocopy and fill out one worksheet for each activity.)

Name of hobby, organization, or club (location) _____

_____

_____

_____

_____

Dates _____

Title/position (officer/member) _____

Elected (yes/no) _____

Accomplishments _____

_____

_____

_____

_____

_____

_____

_____

Work-related skills acquired _____

_____

_____

_____

_____

_____

_____

_____

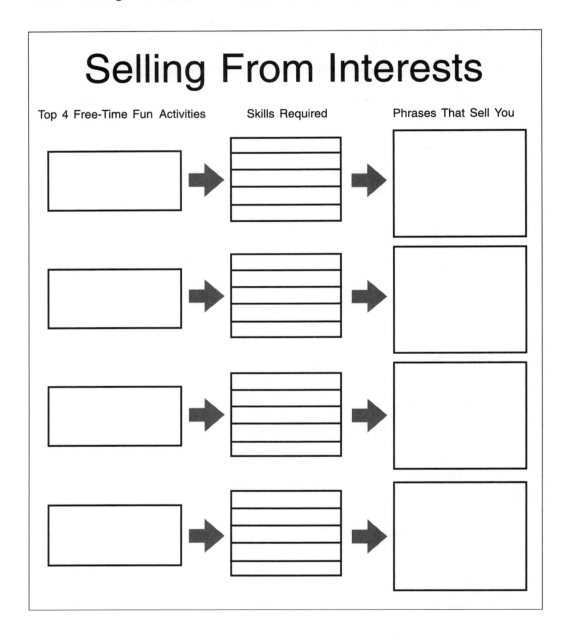

Selling From Interests

Top 4 Free-Time Fun Activities   Skills Required   Phrases That Sell You

Selling From Strengths

Ten Adjectives That Describe Your Strengths

_____   _____

_____   _____

_____   _____

_____   _____

_____   _____

Five Things Others Say You Do Well

Qualifications

What they are, how you got them, and why they're valuable

What	How
Your occupation Your skills	How you acquired this qualification
What: *Network Engineer* ▶	How: *Completed CNA & CNE certification* ▶
What: *Word Processing Applications* ▶	How: *Night school classes* ▶
What: *Spanish Fluency* ▶	How: *Major in college* ▶
What: *Leadership Skills* ▶	How: *Elected President of college senior class* ▶
What: ▶	How: ▶
What: ▶	How: ▶
What: ▶	How: ▶

Why It Matters

So what? What benefits does this qualification bring your target employer?

Why: *Computer network will operate with less downtime*

Why: *Productive immediately*

Why: *Spanish-speaking customers will find it easier to deal with company*

Why: *Can provide guidance to new summer interns*

Why:

Why:

Why:

Achievements Summary

For (target position) _____

****

Work Experience

    Position title

    Company

    Notable Activities

    Results Achieved

    Key Benefits to Employer

    Which Skills Were Used

    How This Achievement Relates to Target Position

Education and Training

    I Learned (Skill) _____ in

    (Name of Course) _____

    How the Skill Relates to Target Position

Part III
Writing RedHot Cover Letters

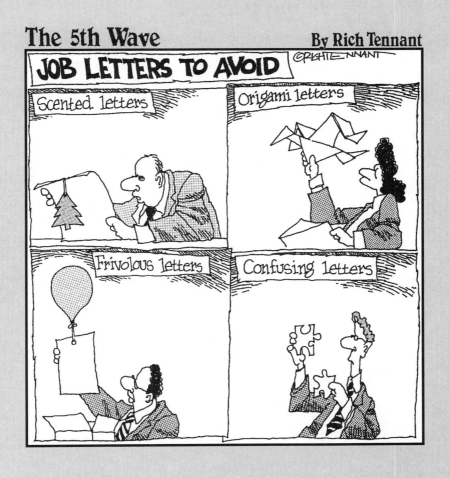

The 5th Wave   By Rich Tennant

JOB LETTERS TO AVOID   ©RICHTENNANT

Scented letters

Origami letters

Frivolous letters

Confusing letters

In this part . . .

*W*hen you write a cover letter, you want to display all the charm and personality of a letter to a friend, all the grammar and intellect of a prize-winning essay, and all the heat-seeking skills of a RedHot job candidate. The trick, of course, is to combine these three parts of you into a cover letter that lands you the interview.

This part is here to help you jump through the cover letter-writing hoops. You'll find a great deal of information on common grammar errors. You'll get tips on writing a dazzling opening line. And you'll work through a RedHot Cover Letter checklist to make sure that your cover letter truly covers all the best aspects of YOU. A good cover letter can be a gift to an employer in need. Read on to find out how to help your future employer unwrap a present in an envelope — your cover letter.

Chapter 7

Language that Snap-Crackle-Pops

● ●

In This Chapter

▶ Writing for a specific reader

▶ Selling yourself with style and verve

▶ Help! Reach into this grammar first-aid kit

● ●

*V*isualize your reader and write specifically for that reader. Speaking directly to your reader may seem obvious, but this tenet is one of the most overlooked aspects of effective writing. Writing to a real person makes your letter more personable and interesting to read. It shows you have considered your reader and want that person to understand what you have to say.

If your blank sheet of paper is beginning to look like the place where you'll spend eternity, rip a page from a magazine featuring a picture of someone who could be reading your letter, tape the picture to your computer, and write to that specific person. Who cares if you select a picture of a conservative middle-aged man with gray hair, when in reality the reader of your letter is a vivacious, young woman with bouncing red curls? No matter. The process — the visualization allowing you to target a particular human being — is what counts.

Refreshing Your Language

Once I asked a friend who writes and publishes career books if he genuinely likes to write. "Well, no," he responded, "I like to have written."

That sentiment sums everything up for many who do almost anything to avoid writing but who know that they can't escape this lifetime without learning to write certain things — a cover letter is one of those things.

Make this task easier for yourself not only by reviewing a few rules of grammar, but also by reminding yourself to answer the big "So why?" and "So what?" questions in every letter.

Why are you writing?

So why are you writing? Never assume the purpose of your letter is obvious to your reader. You are writing a cover letter — or another type of job letter — ultimately aimed at employment.

If you are writing a cover letter, you want to land an interview. Say so. Try to maintain control by saying that you will be in touch at a specified time to see if an interview is possible. When this approach seems impractical, like when you respond to a blind recruitment ad, close with a benefit you offer — "My former boss describes me as the best multimedia designer in the state. Can we talk?"

If you are writing another type of job letter, tell your reader exactly what you want. Leave no room for guessing.

What does it matter?

For each sentence you write, ask yourself, "So what?" What does this information mean to my reader — a benefit gained, a loss avoided, a promise of good things to come — what? Don't, for instance, merely list a bunch of skills and achievements — what good will those skills do for the person who reads your letter?

Must you always interpret the benefit for the reader of your skills and achievements?

> ✔ Yes, if a ghost of an outside chance exists that the benefits of your skills and achievements are not evident to the reader. The former chancellor of a university in Berlin may need to explain how her skills relate to the running of a university in Ireland.

> ✔ No, if the listing of your skills and achievements is so strong that an eighth grader will get the message. The former President of the United States would not need to explain how his skills relate to the running of a university in the U.S.

For more illustrations of when you must interpret your benefits, look over the model cover letters in Chapters 11 and 12.

Getting in the habit of asking yourself "So what?" boosts the power of your job letters by 100 percent.

Technical versus nontechnical language

Tailor your language to your reader. If you are an engineer writing to another engineer, then use technical language. If you're an engineer writing to a director of human resources, your reader may not understand technical engineering language, so you need to explain any technical terms in simple, everyday language. If you use technical language when writing to a nontechnical person, you're likely to lose your reader.

Concise but thorough

Your reader may be pressed for time, so you should aim to write a concise but thorough cover letter. You may wonder how being both concise and thorough at the same time is possible. Think of this task as giving a lengthy explanation in as few words as possible. Tell your reader as much about you as you can, but don't make your reader wade through extra words and unnecessary details. Consider the following example:

> *I am a person who believes that the values of fervent dedication, cooperative teamwork, dynamic leadership, and adaptive creativity really make up the cornerstones and are the crucial components of any totally successful sales venture.*

Revised for concise but thorough language, the same sentence now reads:

> *Dedication, teamwork, leadership, and creativity are essential to successful sales.*

Use short, simple words, sentences, and paragraphs. Avoid cramming too many ideas into each paragraph. Logically break long paragraphs into several short ones.

Simple, direct language

The goal of any written work is communication. To make that communication easier, use simple, direct language that gets your message across clearly and concisely. Don't use your thesaurus to find words that may make you look smarter and the recipient of your letter dumber. Instead, use your thesaurus to find the word best suited for the meaning you want to achieve. For example,

> *Eschew superfluous obfuscation*

makes more sense translated as

> *Avoid unnecessary complication*

For more direct language, use specific terms; avoid generalities or vague descriptions. Use numbers, measures, and facts — detailed information — rather than unquantified descriptions. Consider the following example:

> *I saved the company a fortune when I instituted a new system for scheduling.*

Now read the same example revised for specifics:

> *I saved the company more than one million dollars in production when I instituted a new system for production scheduling.*

Table 7-1 provides a list of word baggage to avoid and RedHot words to replace them.

Table 7-1	RedHot Replacements
Instead of	*Write*
able	can
about	approximately (be precise)
above	this/that
absolutely	(eliminate)
according to	said
ad	advertisement
advanced planning	planning
advise	write/perform
aforementioned	this/that
ahold	reach/get hold of/obtain
alright	all right
along the lines of	like
alot	a lot
a lot of	many/much
arrived at the conclusion	concluded
as per	according to
as to whether	whether
at a later date	later
at the present writing	now
at the present time	now

Instead of	Write
attached hereto	attached/enclosed
attached herein	attached/enclosed
bachelor's degree	bachelor's
bad	poor/inappropriate
beneficial success	success
better than	more than
between each	between every/beside each
between you and I	between you and me
bit	(eliminate)
but however	but *or* however
but that	that
cannot but	(eliminate)
can't hardly	can hardly
city of San Francisco	San Francisco
close proximity	close *or* proximity
close scrutiny	scrutiny
close to the point of	close to
cohese	cohere
concerning the matter of	concerning/about
concerning	about
continue on	continue
disregardless	regardless
due to the fact that	because
each and every	each *or* every
end result	result
entirely completed	completed
equally as	as *or* equally
estimated at about	estimated at
every other	every (second) day
ex-	former
fewer in number	fewer

(continued)

Table 7-1 *(continued)*

Instead of	*Write*
file away	file
for the purpose of	for
for the reason that	because
for your information	(eliminate)
gather together	gather *or* together
good success	success
he is a man who...	he ...
he or she	he
idea	belief/theory/plan
i.e./e.g.	that is/for example
if and when	if *or* when
important essentials	essentials
in accordance with a request	as you requested
inasmuch as	since/because
in connection with	about/concerning
in excess of	over/more than
in order to	to
in respect to the matter of	about/regarding
in spite of	despite
in the amount of	for
in the area of	about
in the field of medicine	in medicine
in this day and age	now/today
irregardless	regardless
join together	join *or* together
keep continuing	continue
kindly	please/very much
kind of	rather/somewhat
known to be	is/are

Instead of	*Write*
know-how	knowledge/understanding
large portion/number of	most of/many
last but not least	(eliminate)
like for	like
like to have	(eliminate)
lot/lots	(eliminate)
love	(eliminate)
magnitude	importance/significance
master's degree	master's
more essential	essential
more perfect	perfect
more specially	specially
more unique	unique
most carefully	(eliminate)
most certainly	(eliminate)
mutual cooperation	cooperation
mutual teamwork	teamwork
near future	soon
needless to say	(eliminate)
new innovation	innovation
new record	record
now pending	pending
of between/of from	of
optimize	increase efficiency
outline in detail	outline *or* detail
overall	comprehensive/final
per	(eliminate)
per diem	daily
per annum	yearly
period of	for
plan ahead	plan

(continued)

Table 7-1 *(continued)*

Instead of	Write
please be advised	(eliminate)
point in time	now
presently	now/soon
qualified expert	qualified *or* expert
rather unique	unique
reason is because	because
reason why	because
regarding	about
represent	composed/made up of
respecting	about
revert back	revert
scrutinize closely	scrutinize
seem	(be more specific)
seriously consider	consider
several	many/numerous
should/would/must *of*	should/would/must *have*
spell out in detail	spell out *or* detail
subject	(be more specific)
subject matter	subject
subsequent to	after
sufficient enough	sufficient *or* enough
take for example	for example
take into consideration	consider
target	goal/objective/quota
thank you in advance	(eliminate)
that	(eliminate if possible)
there is/are/was/were	(eliminate)
true facts	facts
try and	try to
unknown	unidentified/undisclosed

Instead of	Write
unthinkable	unlikely/impossible
very unique	unique
was a former	was/is a former
way in which	way
whatsoever at all	whatsoever
with the exception of	except/except for
yet	(eliminate if possible)
you know	(eliminate)

Active voice versus passive voice

Active voice uses verbs to indicate a motion or action. Using active voice makes your writing more dynamic and interesting. With active voice, you identify who does what — and how!

On the other hand, passive voice (as in this sentence) is characterized by passive verbs and is a description of a state of existence. Because passive voice is generally weak, avoiding it is beneficial. Some passive verbs include be, is, was, were, are, seem, has, and been.

Revising the above paragraph for active voice results in the following:

> *Passive voice, on the other hand, characterized by passive verbs, indicates a state of existence. Because passive voice generally weakens writing, try to avoid it.*

Passive voice just sits there, without vigor and without action. Take responsibility for your achievements. Be active.

Past/present tense

For the most part, use present tense as you're writing. After all, your letter is something you're creating now. When you refer to accomplishments or achievements, use past tense.

When your resume says you are currently employed (199X - Present), remember to use the present tense if you refer to your current job in a cover letter. If you slip and use the past tense, the reader may assume you've left the job and are pretending to be currently employed.

Fundamentals of Grammar and Punctuation

Grammar slips sink jobs. Many employers see language skills as an important aspect of potential job performance, and nothing says language skills like attention to grammar and punctuation. To help you over some areas that many cover letter writers find tricky, here is a brief overview of frequently made mistakes and how to correct them.

Sentence fragments

Sentence fragments signal an incomplete thought. They neglect an essential component. For example,

Although I work in Detroit, making $200 an hour.

This fragment is missing the subsequent subject and verb needed to finish the "while I work . . ."

To test your sentences, speak each one aloud, out of context. Imagine walking up to someone and saying that sentence. Would the sentence make sense, or is something missing? If so, add the missing information.

Although I work in Detroit, making $200 an hour, I prefer to work in Atlanta to be near my family.

Run-on sentences

Run-on sentences are two complete sentences written as one. For example,

I finished writing my cover letter, it's great!

This run-on should read:

I finished writing my cover letter. It's great!

Each sentence contains a complete thought and should stand on its own.

Run-on sentences stand out as grammatical errors and signal either a lack of attention in English 101 or lack of precision in your editing skills. If you don't care enough about your cover letter to make sure that it's grammatically perfect, a potential employer may wonder how much you'll care about precision in your job.

Dangling participles

Dangling participles are words ending in *-ing* that modify the wrong subject. For example,

>Running across the water, we saw a huge water beetle.

This sentence literally means that we saw a water beetle while we were running across the water — a rather incredible situation. You should revise the sentence to read:

>We saw a huge water beetle running across the water.

Dangling participles undoubtedly cause chuckles, but they indicate imprecision or lack of care, qualities no potential employer appreciates in a prospective employee.

Misplaced modifiers

Like dangling participles, misplaced modifiers modify the wrong subject, often resulting in hilarious miscommunications. For example,

>Ben taught the dog, an inveterate womanizer, to bark at all blonde women.

The dog is an inveterate womanizer? Probably not. Revised, this sentence makes more sense:

>Ben, an inveterate womanizer, taught the dog to bark at all blonde women.

Semicolons

Semicolons can be tricky, so you should probably avoid them if you don't feel comfortable using them. In essence, semicolons are weak periods; they indicate a separation between two complete sentences that are so closely related they "shouldn't" be separated by a period.

As you can see, this definition is not too specific. Because no definite rule exists for this use of semicolons, you may simply use periods between every sentence. You won't break any rules, and you'll avoid using semicolons incorrectly.

The only rigid rule for semicolons is as follows: When you introduce a list of complete sentences using a colon, separate each sentence with a semi-colon. For example,

I accomplished the following: I networked all the computers, company-wide; I designed a new system for scheduling; and I broke the world's record in typing speed.

Again, you can avoid this use of semicolons in your cover letter by placing each item on a separate line set-off by bullets. No punctuation is necessary at the end of each line. For example,

I accomplished the following:

- *I networked all the computers, company-wide*

- *I designed a new system for scheduling*

- *I broke the world's record in typing speed*

Punctuation in parenthetical expressions

If a parenthetical expression occurs in the middle or at the end of a sentence, place the punctuation outside of the parentheses. Some examples include the following:

Cover letters are essential (see Chapter 1).

Cover letters (and resumes) are essential.

Cover letters (and resumes), essential to the job search, are easy to write.

Question marks and exclamation points, when part of a parenthetical expression occurring in the middle of a sentence, are the exception to this rule. Some examples include the following:

The interview (or was it an inquisition?) was a disaster.

My cover letter (a masterpiece!) took 4 hours to write.

If a parenthetical expression stands alone as a sentence, place the punctuation inside of the parentheses. For example,

(I will discuss these skills in a moment.)

Commas in a series

Whenever you have a series of terms separated by commas, use a comma after the next-to-last term for clarity. Some examples include the following:

Cover letters, resumes, and interviews make up part of the job-search process.

Dear Mr. Barnes, Ms. Collins, and Ms. Schultz

This technique is called the *serial comma*. Serial commas are not used in newspapers because they slow down reading. Be consistent in your use of commas. Don't use a serial comma in one paragraph, and no serial comma in another that calls for one.

Hyphenating words for clarity

When you use two words together as a description of another word, use a hyphen. Examples include:

> next-to-last job
>
> sure-fire solution
>
> long-range plan

To test whether you should use a hyphen, take out one of the descriptive terms and see if the description still makes sense. For example,

> next-to-last job

without one descriptive term, becomes

> to last job

Doesn't make sense, does it? Because the three words "next to last" cannot be used individually as a description and still make sense, you need hyphens between them.

The same rule applies for two nouns used together to express a single idea. Examples include:

> light-year
>
> life-cycle

For greatest accuracy, check a dictionary.

As with most things in English, you find exceptions: Words ending in *-ly* do not need a hyphen when used as part of a description unless they are used with a present participle (a verb ending in *-ing*). For example,

> professionally written resume

descriptively accurate cover letter

friendly-sounding cover letter

Abbreviations

Only use abbreviations if you have previously written out what the abbreviation stands for. For example, do not write UCSD if you have not previously written University of California, San Diego (UCSD). Never assume that your reader knows or will be able to figure out what an abbreviation stands for.

Some exceptions: Abbreviations such as AIDS, LSD, and DNA are so well known that they do not have to be defined. Also, some technical jargons commonly use abbreviations. In that case, write to your reader. If your reader will understand the abbreviation, use it.

If you're writing to a nontechnical person who may not understand, write an abbreviation out the first time you use it, perhaps with a brief description. If the abbreviation is a technical term normally not spelled out, provide the abbreviation with a brief description. For example,

GSI, a programming language

LYCOS, a search engine

Consecutive numbers

When you use two numbers in a row, avoid confusion by writing out the shorter of the two numbers:

six 9-person teams

Or revise your sentence to separate the numbers:

six teams of nine people

Numbers at the beginning of a sentence

Whenever a sentence begins with a number, write out the number rather than using numerals. Better yet, revise the sentence so the number does not appear at the beginning.

Commas

In general, use commas any place you would pause if you read the sentence aloud. If you're a person who pauses often while speaking, this suggestion probably won't work for you. My advice is to ask several people to read your letter for punctuation and grammar, and follow their suggestions. Or get a good punctuation guide and follow it.

Capitalization of trade names

Trade names, like Band-Aid, Kleenex, or Xerox should be capitalized. Avoid using these trade names to refer to a class of things or to an action. For example,

> I need a Band-Aid.

Use bandage unless you specifically want the brand-name product.

> I need to Xerox some papers

is also technically incorrect. Write

> I need to photocopy some papers.

Capitalizing for importance

Resist the urge to Capitalize words to make them Stand out as Important. Doing so looks Contrived and Juvenile. It's also wrong.

Capitalize titles of departments, companies, and agencies

Any official name of a company, department, agency, division, or organization should be capitalized. Examples include:

> U.S. Department of Labor
>
> Department of Safety

Don't capitalize words such as department, company, or organization when used as a general word rather than as part of a specific title. For example,

> I work for a division of Chrysler.

Table 7-2 provides a handy chart to help you through the grammatical thicket.

Table 7-2	RedHot Grammar Guide		
Error Term	**Definition of Term**	**Don't Do This**	**Do This**
Subject-verb disagreement	Subject and verb don't agree, resulting in a grammatically incorrect sentence.	Our team, as well as the company, *value* ambition.	Our team, as well as the company, *values* ambition.
Active voice vs. passive voice	Active voice relates an action (good); passive voice relates a state of existence (bad).	*I was trained* in all aspects of public relations.	U.C.I. *trained me* in all aspects of public relations.
Sentence cants, fragment	Phrase lacks a subject and/or verb, revealing an incomplete thought.	*Unlike some applicants.*	Unlike some applicants, *I bring* talent and diversity.
Run-on sentence	Contains more than one complete thought; may lack punctuation.	Every writer knows how important grammar is, *I* know you really value marketing, and sales skills, in your business correspondence.	Every writer knows the importance of grammar. *I also* understand you value marketing and sales skills in your business correspondence.
Subject-pronoun disagreement	Pronouns don't agree with subject, resulting in confusing or easily misunderstood sentence.	When *someone* reads, *they* should pay attention to details.	When *someone* reads, *he (or she)* should pay attention to details. *Or,* When *people* read, they should pay attention to details.
Misplaced modifiers	Incorrect placement of a description of one subject in a sentence with two subjects; result is confusion.	Falling more than 500 feet, we watched the daredevil bungee jump off a cliff.	We watched the daredevil bungee jump, falling more than 500 feet off a cliff.

Organizing for RedHot Impact

Poor organization is one of the big reasons people's cover letters fail to make the RedHot category. Poor planning results in poor organization. Start with a rough outline that identifies the contents and how the contents will be organized on your cover letter.

Most publishers require an author to write a table of contents — the TOC (pronounced tee-o-see). The TOC shows how the book will be organized. This requirement keeps the author from wandering away from a logical development of the topic. The TOC can be changed as the book develops, but its preparation serves as a map when you begin writing. Review Chapter 8, describing the anatomy of a cover letter, and then draft your own TOC.

Formats for organization

Following are several formats to suggest how your letter can be organized. Any organizational format can be used with any occupation.

Problem/Solution

The problem/solution format starts with "Here's the problem" and ends with "Here's how I solved it." Case histories and success stories blossom in this favorite format for cover letters and resumes.

Inverted pyramid

News stories use this format. You start with a lead paragraph summarizing the story, with the following paragraphs presenting facts in order of decreasing importance. In your cover letter, you state a comprehensive goal, career desire, or position at the beginning, and then provide specific examples in the following paragraphs to support your aim.

Deductive order

Much like the inverted pyramid, the deductive order format starts with a generalization and ends with specific examples supporting the generalization. For example, you can start by making a general statement about a skill. Then support that statement with facts.

Inductive order

Begin your letter with a story or anecdote and then lead the reader to the conclusion that can be drawn from the story or anecdote. You explain how that story or anecdote supports your ability to succeed at the job you've targeted.

List

Separate your letter into distinct points and set the points off with headings, bullets, or numbers. Put the most important point first. This format is especially effective for enumerating skills or achievements. This format is usually combined within another format (such as the T-letter of Chapter 3) for extra punch.

Three blazing tips

1. Highlight short sentences and lists with bullets, asterisks, or em dashes. For example,

   • Won Orchid award for building

   * Won Orchid award for building

   – Won Orchid award for building

2. Start with a short quote that reflects the employer's policies or values.

3. Reword portions of the employer's mission statement or other documents and work these phrases into your letter as you describe your skills, work ethic, and values.

Ask yourself, Why?

When you finish writing your letter, read it over just to check its organization. When you read it, each line should seem to fit into the other. You shouldn't really notice that a new sentence has begun. You should feel "prepared" for everything that you're about to read.

To avoid jarring the reader with an abrupt change of subject, ask yourself, "Why did I place this sentence or paragraph after the one before it?" If the answer is not obvious in your letter, the flow of your text is probably choppy and unclear to the reader. Analyze what's not working and rewrite until the letter reads smoothly.

Chapter 8

Dissecting Cover Letter Anatomy

● ●

In This Chapter

▶ Connecting the parts of a RedHot cover letter

▶ Writing a letter that says "Hire Me!"

▶ Taking a quiz — Do you know your cover letter's anatomy?

● ●

*I*n case you've forgotten or never learned the parts of a job letter, review these building blocks.

Contact Information

Your address, telephone number, e-mail address, and URL (Internet World Wide Web address) appear first on the letter. As you can see from the sample letters in Chapters 12 and 13, you can place your address in the middle or on either side of the page. Just make sure that your URL is on a line of its own.

You have a choice about where to place your name. You can either place it (preferably in larger letters) above your address, or you can type it below your signature. The only stipulation: don't put it in both places. It's a waste.

Computer-friendly cover letters place the telephone number, e-mail address, and URL address on separate lines below your residential address for better scanning. You can also separate two items on the same line.

Date Line and Inside Address

Place the date two lines below your contact information, and place the inside address two lines below the date. Aligned with the left side of the page, enter the name of the person to whom you're writing (with Mr. or Ms. designation), followed on the next line by the company name, followed on the next lines by the address. If you know the position the receiver of your letter holds, include that information on the same line as the receiver's name or on the following line.

On the right side of the page, aligned with the inside address information, you can include a line labeled *RE:* to highlight the reason for correspondence.

Salutation

Your salutation says, "Hello!" in the form of *Dear Person-Who-Can-Hire-Me*. It's like the eye contact that establishes a connection and begins the dialogue. Do your best to identify the person who will read your letter, and address that person directly. Not only does your reader appreciate being addressed by name, but also, this personal bit separates your letter from the ones written by people who didn't take the time to do a little research into the company. Chapter 2 gives you some tips on how to go about finding the name.

If you can't uncover the name of the hiring manager, write *Dear Employer* or *Good Morning*. It's cheerful and feels more personal than *Dear Sir or Madam* or *To Whom It May Concern*. Remember to complete the salutation with a colon (:) to indicate more information to come.

Because no one enjoys reading mail addressed to a generic person (remember all the junk mail you've trashed addressed *Dear Resident?*), try, try, try to discover the name of your reader. It's courteous, it takes initiative, and it indicates genuine interest in the company and, most importantly, in the job.

Introduction

Your introduction should grab your reader's attention immediately. As the "head" of your letter, it appeals to the head of your reader, sparking interest that will compel your reader to keep reading. It subtly says "Read Me!" and states the purpose of the letter.

All sorts of rules have been given for ways to start your cover letter. Some say "Don't start with I." Others advise shock value and creativity, a risky approach for some. The most important rule is to engage the reader's interest. What does the reader need in an employee that you can draw attention to from the get-go? For more information on RedHot opening lines, check out Chapter 9.

Body

The body of your letter provides essential information that the employer should know about you — skills, achievements, and quantified statements about your past accomplishments. These skills may double as the interest-generating element of your letter as well. Unless your cover letter also serves as your resume, the body of your cover letter should be one to six paragraphs in length for eye-friendly appeal.

The body should include a brief background summary of your relevant experience. I suggest including it somewhat like this: "As an accountant at Donne Brothers Company, I accomplished the following: _____ " This is information that the reader can get from your resume so don't spend too much time on it in your letter. But don't be tempted to leave it out. Without this key selling point, your reader may never get to your resume.

The information that you include in the body of your cover letter gives tangible evidence of your potential contribution to an employer. It provides your reader with facts to digest and satisfies hunger for a valuable employee. Make sure these facts are tasty, enticing your reader to devour your resume and call you in for an interview.

Conclusion

The last leg of your letter aims to stimulate action on your behalf. It gets your reader's blood pumping and legs moving toward the telephone to call you before anyone else does.

Motivating your reader to action requires a sincere "thank you for your time and consideration" and a contact date. Always tell your reader when you will call (no more than one week) to confirm receipt of your letter and resume and coordinate a time for an interview. Including this information insures that you'll act; you promised. Your word is on the line. If you call, a potential employer certainly can't ignore you — someone at least will have to move to answer the telephone. And if the news is not good, at least you're not home waiting by the telephone for a call that never comes.

Closing, Signature, and Enclosure Line

The closing section says "Good-bye." It's the handshake before parting, sincere and warm with promise of meetings to come. *Sincerely* and *Very truly yours* are the most popular, but other choices include *Best regards, Warm regards*, and *Sincerely yours*. Don't forget to put a comma after your closing line.

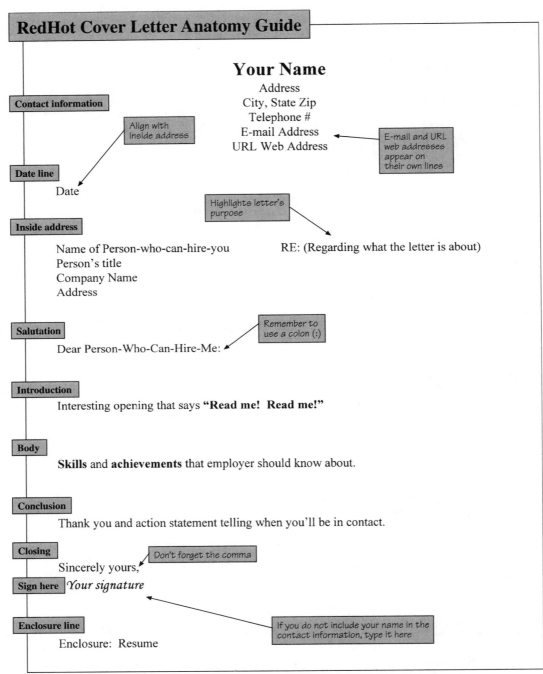

RedHot Cover Letter Anatomy Guide

Contact information

Your Name
Address
City, State Zip
Telephone #
E-mail Address
URL Web Address

Align with inside address

E-mail and URL web addresses appear on their own lines

Date line

Date

Highlights letter's purpose

Inside address

Name of Person-who-can-hire-you
Person's title
Company Name
Address

RE: (Regarding what the letter is about)

Salutation

Remember to use a colon (:)

Dear Person-Who-Can-Hire-Me:

Introduction

Interesting opening that says **"Read me! Read me!"**

Body

Skills and **achievements** that employer should know about.

Conclusion

Thank you and action statement telling when you'll be in contact.

Closing

Don't forget the comma

Sincerely yours,

Sign here *Your signature*

Enclosure line

If you do not include your name in the contact information, type it here

Enclosure: Resume

Don't forget to sign off. If your name *doesn't appear* in your contact information, type your name below your signature (four lines below closing) so that there will be no confusion about spelling.

If your penmanship runs to chicken-scratch, try to make your signature legible. Any employer prefers to be able to read what someone hand-writes rather than have to interpret it.

Once you've motivated your reader to action, the enclosure line provides a direction. Indicate everything else that you've sent with your cover letter, such as resumes or portfolios. This line directly follows your typed name or signature.

Now Test Yourself

Now let's see how much you know. Take the following 40-question true-false quiz which tests some of the knowledge presented in this chapter as well as your general knowledge of cover letters (see Chapters 1, 2, and 7 for more information). Place an X under T (for true) or F (for false).

Your RedHot Cover Letter Anatomy Quiz (Part 1)

	True (T)	False (F)
Contact Information		
1. Includes your nickname(s)		
2. Includes your name (no abbreviations)		
3. Includes your direct mailing address(es)		
4. Lists all your e-mail and URL Web addresses on address line		
5. Includes your telephone number and other numbers (pager, message, office) but excludes ex-employer numbers		
6. No parentheses placed around telephone area codes		
Date Line		
7. Date is written in full or in brief (abbreviate or number months)		
8. Date is on its own line two lines below contact information		
Inside Address		
9. Includes recipient's name, spelled correctly, 2 lines under date		
10. Includes recipient's job title + designations, if any (Ph.D., M.D., C.P.A.)		

(continued)

Your RedHot Cover Letter Anatomy Quiz *(continued)*

	True (T)	False (F)
11. Includes recipient's company (spell out acronyms; NASA = National Aeronautics & Space Administration)		
12. May hail multiple readers with "Messrs," "Misses," "Mesdames"		
13. Includes recipient's address		

Salutation

14. Uses "Dear — " "Greetings — " or "Good Morning — " two lines under inside address — greets with friendly tone		
15. Includes designation (Mr., Ms., Dr.)		
16. Ends with semicolon (;)		

Introduction

17. Grabs the reader's attention at once, two lines under salutation		
18. Lists who referred you and objective in first line		
19. Mentions any mutual acquaintances or previous contact		
20. States the position you apply for by job title		
21. Names advertisement (+ publication and date) or contact that led you to apply		
22. Lists your top sales points, experience, credentials, or accomplishments		

Body

23. Lists personal information verbatim from resume		
24. Lists information about you, but targets employer's interests		
25. Details how your qualifications and qualities contribute to employer		
26. Discusses what you didn't like at your last job		
27. Discusses how your skills relate to known job requirements		

	True (T)	False (F)
28. Explains why you apply to this specific employer — what interests you		
29. Discusses your familiarity with the industry, including employer's competitors		
30. Discusses what you stand to gain (financially) by working with this company		
31. You can write as many as six paragraphs or as few as one in the body		
32. Discusses salary history and requirements in detail		
33. Discusses personal issues and money troubles to evoke the reader's sympathy		

Conclusion

34. Thanks the reader for his or her time and interest		
35. Motivates the reader by asking employer to call you at a specific time or date		
36. Initiates action by mentioning that you look forward to discussing the position further with the reader		
37. Tells the reader what follow-up measures you will take		

Closing

38. Two lines below last sentence, uses a complimentary closure statement like "Sincerely yours,"		
39. When enclosing a resume, "Enclosure: Resume" appears at the bottom-left corner of the cover letter		
40. Signature appears at bottom in blue or black ink		

Understanding Your Score

Most of the statements above are true, however, false statements may have sounded true, so I will comment only on false statements. If you got 35 right out of 40, you're RedHot material. If you only got 30 right, you should review this chapter as well as Chapters 1, 2, and 7, and the samples in Part IV.

Here are explanations of the False statements:

1. Nicknames detract from a professional image.

4. E-mail and URL Web addresses each need their own lines (or be widely separated by white space on the same line) because computer scanners can't distinguish them from other number patterns, such as telephone/address numbers. (See Chapters 1 and 8.)

6. Telephone area codes appear in parentheses, for computer scanners to distinguish them from other numbers in the heading. (See Chapter 1.)

12. Messrs., Mesdames, and Misses went out of print with the manual typewriter. Use the name of each addressee (+ designation) when possible. (See Part IV.)

16. Easily confused with the colon, the semicolon (;) divides a two-part sentence. The colon follows salutations to flag more information to follow. (See Chapter 7.)

23. Personal information reinforces your chances for an interview only when it is somehow relevant to the position; never repeat your resume in the letter, because your letter's main focus is to snag the reader's interest in reading the resume, not to give away the resume itself. (See Chapters 1, 2, and 8.)

26. Omit all negative information. Complaining about your last job looks long-winded and unprofessional on paper and may lead to assumptions that you are difficult to work with. (See Chapter 2.)

30. Address the employer's financial interests, not yours. (See Chapter 1.)

32. Salary issues are complex. See Chapter 16 to understand them better. Try to save salary talk until the interview, but if you respond to employer's request for salary history or requirements, say as little as possible and speak in ranges: "Am in the $XX to $XX range (Confidential)."

33. People are not hired out of sympathy. Let positive attributes and qualifications speak for you. (See Chapter 1.)

35. Asking the reader to contact you is unrealistic. (See the sample, subtle substitutes in Part IV.)

Chapter 9

Igniting a Spark with the Opening Line

In This Chapter

▶ Writing opening statements that stand out from the crowd

▶ Examples of hot properties

▶ Plug-in-the-blank statements to help you get started

▶ Loser opening statements

Suppose you receive a letter that begins

> *Time flies when you're having fun.*

That oldie probably won't entice your reading interest.

But suppose you receive a letter that begins

> *As Muppet Kermit the Frog says, "Time's fun when you're having flies."*

That line is different. That line is funny. That opening lassoes your eyes, roping you into reading further. You keep scanning to find out what message such a whimsical letter could possibly be communicating.

I'm not suggesting you start job letters with frog quotes or other whimsical statements, but I am pointing out that you must work to grab attention. Build a fire under your cover letter by opening with words that intrigue, words that excite, words that zing!

Your opening words make your first impression. And you know what they say about that — you never get a second chance to make a good first impression. The old standard "Enclosed please find my resume in response to your newspaper advertisement" (and its clones) adds no distinction or lure to your message. The sentence just lies there — instead of a sparkler, the tired words read more like a fizzled-out cherry bomb.

Learn to write openings that fire up the reader and move the reader along without wasting tons of time. Interviewers are overloaded — whole days are a blur for them, and they have no spare minutes to decipher what it is you can do for them.

Consider the harried interviewer pouring over an arcane or boring cover letter: "Why am I wading through this slush? I'm not. Let's sail this sucker right into the trash with the other gibberish."

If your cover letter starts off with tired blood, your reader will likely be too bored to keep on reading.

Two Tips to Open Your Letter

The best information to put into your opening line is a name: the name of the letter's recipient or of a mutual friend. Name dropping virtually guarantees that your letter will be read. To get attention, nothing beats the coattails of someone the letter's recipient likes or respects.

Even if the gatekeeping clerical staff doesn't know the names you drop from Adam's house cat, you'll increase your letter's chances of landing on the right desk.

The second-best information to put into the opening line is a clear statement of what you want, followed by the benefits you offer — qualifications you have that directly relate to the qualities the hiring company seeks. Skills are mother's milk to opening statements on cover letters.

Don't waste space in your opening lines by citing the source of a job opening notice — "I saw your ad in the *KoKoMo Express* last Sunday." Handle that in the "RE:" line in the upper, right-hand quadrant (see sample cover letters in Chapter 11).

A Sampling of Sizzling Sells

Having trouble launching your first letter? I rounded up some of the best opening lines I could find — from real cover letters — and present them here to inspire you.

- "During your visit to UCSB last fall, I had the pleasure of hearing you address the issue of FuelCO oil rigs off the coast of Santa Barbara."
- "We acknowledged and discussed my diverse background when I assisted you through the Internet; I enclose my resume for your consideration."
- "Since you will soon be working on photo sessions for the Spring catalog, I have enclosed my resume and portfolio to show just how ideal my background in photography and design is for your marketing strategies."

- ✔ "Juliette Nagy mentioned your company has opened a division of sporting goods and suggested I contact you."

- ✔ "Your speech was inspiring, Miss Rogers. Soon I will have completed my master of arts in physical therapy, just in time for your entry-level openings in the PT ward."

- ✔ "Chaim Isenberg of the Grenwich and Co. accounting firm suggested I contact you regarding opportunities in your warehouse division in Champagne."

What makes these opening lines so great? Some mention names. Some connect to a common experience. Some reveal in-depth knowledge of the company involved. All show the letter writer as a person who cares enough to give time and attention to the presentation made in this self-marketing tool.

Exercises to Start Your Motor

Following is a series of plug-in-the-word statements to help you get started.

Name value phrases

As noted earlier, name value phrases help you connect your name with the interviewer's through the use of mutual contacts or associations. They give the interviewer one reason to pay attention to your application and a point of reference. If you're naming a person known to the interviewer, alerting that person to the fact that you're using his or her name is a good idea.

✔ **You know of no job opening but the interviewer requests that you send a resume:**

As you requested in our telephone conversation on (date), I enclose a copy of my resume for your review. A quick reading shows my well-developed skills in (a laundry list of your strongest skill sets).

✔ **You call about a job ad, and someone in the company tells you to send a resume:**

As (name of individual) requested during our telephone conversation on (date), I am including my resume for your review.

✔ **A friend or important person suggests you send a resume:**

On (date), I discussed your opening for (job title) with (so-and-so), who suggested I forward my resume to your office. We discussed the position's priorities; they seem to align perfectly with my education and experience. As my enclosed resume shows, my (a skill) and (an experience) will work great in your position.

✔ **You know the job title but can't reach a person by telephone:**

As your office requested, I am enclosing my resume in application for the (job opening title) opening. I understand your company values (a skill), (a type of experience), and (a work trait), and my experience illustrates such qualifications.

If you can't scrounge up a contact or any other "in," try the following general kinds of RedHots to spice up matches between your qualifications and the employer's requirements.

Power phrases

The following opening lines power through with a direct approach and a strong sell that emphasizes belief in yourself and your strengths.

✔ "I am particularly well-qualified for your position and would enjoy the opportunity to meet with you to explore how I can enhance your organization."

✔ "I was excited to read of your opening for (job opening title) in the (name of publication) on (date). Although we do not share any personal acquaintances, you will see from my enclosed resume that we do share many professional interests and goals, such as (mutual goals). Wanting a more personal introduction, I take the liberty of writing to you directly."

✔ "(So-and-so) thought my resume measures such achievement that he assured me he would pass my resume on to you; in the event it hasn't yet reached you, here's a copy."

✔ "For your convenience, I will keep this letter especially brief. The job you're trying to fill has my name on it, thanks to my qualifications in (skills) and (experience)."

✔ "Your position for (job title) strongly appeals to me, because . . ."

✔ "If a meeting confirms my understanding of your open position (job title), I am confident that with my skills in (name skills), I can make an immediate and valuable contribution to (name of employer)."

You want what I am

Similar to direct-mail advertising, this pair of starters sells from the first sentence by directly linking your qualifications with those the firm is in need of.

✔ "I understand that your firm is in search of individuals with (skills) and (qualifications); don't you love finding the perfect match? In reviewing my resume, you will find that I possess all the attributes of that perfect match, from (skills) to (experience or attributes). I am delighted to learn of your job opening, because I have been searching for a company exactly like yours to make real use of my experience."

✔ "Will your (department) reach its (company goal), or will it always (current company problem)? You'll never know without the best person for the job to follow through for you."

Cut to the chase

These opening statements show an awareness of the employer's need for time and efficiency.

✔ "My background demonstrates the skills you require in (name of position)."

✔ "As my resume shows, I have substantial experience in (field/position/ skill)."

✔ "As we discussed earlier, my extensive professional experience can benefit any employer. However, (company name) is of special interest to me because . . . ."

✔ "After developing skills in (appropriate to employer, list top skills, accomplishments from cooperative education or student job experience, or make connection between course work and research), as a graduating senior, I have begun to search for a position in (company/industry). I will graduate (date)."

Or

"After developing skills in (appropriate to employer, list top skills, accomplishments from cooperative education or student job experience, or make connection between course work and research), I recently graduated from (name of educational institution) and am searching for a position in (company/industry)."

✔ "I look forward to meeting with you to further discuss my background and to show you some of the (skills) that I have developed."

Network news phrases

You may not know of any job openings, but others in your field do. Don't be afraid to approach fellow members of professional organizations, friends of friends, or other people you know or are known to for help in your job search. Most people are happy to help if they can, and employers appreciate having a strong applicant pool from which to choose. Following are examples of some approaches you might use in asking for help.

✔ "If any opportunities come to your attention in (field or job title), I would appreciate your informing me. You can expect a call from me on (date)."

✔ "I appreciate any advice and/or referrals that you could pass on to me."

Broadcast letter phrases

The broadcast letter is sent to a variety of places in what is essentially a fishing expedition. This approach is not the best because it is not targeted. But it is a frequently employed tool and one that adds to your arsenal of techniques for finding your best job.

✔ "Among my qualifications, I am a (name your top attribute) aspiring to join a dynamic firm, such as yours, that could benefit from an individual who consistently contributes 150%."

✔ "Last year I earned (dollar amount) for (previous employer). I am confident my experience in (areas) could benefit (company applied to) as effectively."

Openings in dispute

Some advisers in cover letter writing suggest the type of opening that could be considered condescending:

✔ "To maintain solid growth, a company must have marketing and sales professionals who can jump on a market before the competition does. My background proves I can do that."

✔ "When a customer calls for a quote, your firm's future is in the hands of the sales staff. I have big hands."

I personally can't support this type of opening, because it presumes to tell the interviewer the interviewer's business. Think of a job seeker stating the obvious about industry needs and developments to a 30-year industry veteran who makes hiring decisions. If you're determined to take this approach, throw in a lot of "as you know" softening language.

Leadoff Strikeouts: Loser Opening Lines

Just as every baseball team needs a RedHot leadoff hitter at the top of the batting order, every cover letter needs a hard-hitting opener at the top of the page. These real-life cover letter leadoff lines never made it to first base.

Comments that follow in quotation marks are from the employer's view.

✔ I was recently let go due to a reduction in force.

Nothing like starting on an upbeat note.

✔ Having recently completed an assignment in the Commonwealth of Independent States (the former Soviet Union), I am interested in pursuing and advancing my career opportunities into this arena.

Arena? What arena? Here . . . There . . . Where?

✔ In most organizations, job performance, whether excellent or inept, doesn't count, as long as you conform and play politics. I believe that performance does count! I have recently been notified by Dunnie Pharmaceuticals that my R&D position will be eliminated in the near future.

Does this translate to: I wasn't much of a team player? Is that why the writer's position is being eliminated?

✔ I am currently in search of a job; I have no particular preference in any area, for as you can see from my included resume, my experience includes a broad range.

One who will take anything masters nothing. As movie pioneer Sam Goldwyn said, 'Include me out.

✔ I am writing in response to the position for a production coordinator advertised in the paper. I am very interested in advancing in my field and making a transition into the aspects of the communications profession described in your ad.

Do you want to advance in your field (which is what?), or do you want to make a transition, or do you want to do the work I need done?

✔ If you or someone you know could use a graphic designer, please pass my resume on to interested parties, or call me as soon as possible.

If you're asking me to be your agent, remember, agents get 15% off the top.

✔ My partner and I are dissolving our business after 15 years of working together. I am interested in a position at Fred & Associates and have enclosed a resume for your review.

A business divorce is rarely just one person's fault: Are you a pain in the patootie? And what is it you want to do for me?

As noted earlier, you don't get a second chance to make a first impression. Make sure that the first impression you make with your cover letter gives the interviewer reason to invite you in, not write you out.

Cover Letter Crimes

The writers of the highly imaginative letters below did not solve the case of the missing job interview. Their efforts are interesting, funny, charming, and amusing. But employers didn't bite. Generally, employers prefer more predictable letters, where your qualifications do the talking. Exceptions: Cover letters for creative fields, such as advertising, public relations or marketing.

The crime of these letters is that their writers put so much effort into them -- with no result. They're like some television commercials: You think they're whacky and cool, but can't seem to recall the name of their product.

Goals on Steroids

A desperate writer branded himself as unfit with the following homey lines: "Throughout my career I have accomplished many goals, yet there is one challenge I have not met. I have played one on one with Michael Jordan and beat him 40 to 5. I skated against Nancy Kerrigan in a competition and won first place. I discovered the cure for cancer and sold it to the government for a modest price. The only thing I have yet to do is work for you."

Repent, Cover Letter Sinner!

From the handwritten sheet of lined notebook paper to the five lines of felt-tip pen scrawl, this applicant shows a deep-seated need to go agnostic:
DEAR CORN CHIP GOD,
I PRAY TO THEE, THAT I MAY SOMEDAY
WORSHIP YOU AT THE HIGHEST LEVEL
BY WORKING FOR UNITED CORN CHIP
COMPANY.   YOUR FAITHFUL SERVANT

Loan Officer Giveaway

This applicant drew herself with arrows pointing to her professional attributes as a loan officer. She gave herself away without making one red cent:
"Strong knees -- holds up under pressure" "shoulders tested to carry a great deal of responsibility" "Quick on her feet -- will go the extra step" "Shiny shoes -- keeps herself neat & clean."

Candidate for Permanent Shore Leave

This applicant revealed both total desperation and low aspirations in one rookie swoop:
"I would lick the decks clean for a month, in order to get hired on with your company. I have been working for small companies since I've been a junior ship engine mechanic; I am ready for a real job."

Begging For a Broken Heart ♥♥♥♥

Red-flagged with homemade graphics of valentine hearts and the company product, corn flakes, this letter arrived on the desk of an un-named human resources director on February 14th:
"I've been a secret admirer of yours for quite some time. You were in my every thought during my college years. Every time I pour milk, all I can see is you. I have never asked another for such commitment, because I've been waiting for a cereal I could stay with forever. I know thousands of suitors are applying for your affection, but their attempts are nothing in my quest to win your approval. Long-distance relationships are hard, and I'd love to see you face-to-face, to demonstrate my sincerity.
Happy Valentine's Day."

Psst! Child Labor is Illegal These Days

Stapled to a fair (not RedHot) letter was a sheet of kindergarten penmanship paper, proving his life goal to be a pilot:

If *I Could* B e An*y*one. Ma*r*k P. I would be a pilot b ecause I like the in**st**er*m*ent pannel. And I like *to* **go** in*s*ided the *c*louds and look **d**own at the states **a** nd look at the cars. It would be ne at be**c**a**u**se th **e** cars would loo k like ants and people would look li*ke* li t*f*le tiny s*p*ects o f dir*t*. I'd like **to** work the radio, I'd li ke to talk to *t*he control *t*ower *a*/so *I'*d like to see h *o*me movies and land th e airp*l*ane o*n* the runway. A nd I'd like to *b*e the *pi*lot for *I*nternational *F*li**g**ht Airl i*n*es. (*W*ri t *ten* w *h*en I was 6)

Fire Discovered, The Wheel is Invented

Top 10 lists in cover letter form, now common, offer outrageous reasons for why applicants should be interviewed:
- From an applicant for a shipping company, "Thinks boxes are sexy and make nice end tables "
- From an applicant to a bottled water company, "We like our water guy."
- From an applicant to an interstate retailer, 'Lives conveniently between Paris hub and Moscow headquarters."
- From an applicant to a cruise ship, "I run the tightest ship in the family business."

Chapter 10

Making Sure You Have the Write Stuff

• •

In This Chapter

▶ Mark your RedHot cover letter checklist

▶ Grade your cover letter before it's sent

• •

*M*ake sure that your letter is not only read, but also becomes your invitation to an interviewing jamboree. Remember, your letter tells an employer what you can do for the company and offers plenty of reasons to meet you.

Your letter speaks about the benefits you bring to the job: your expertise, your mastery of technology, your personal qualities, your willingness to arrive early and stay late, your thoughts on saving the company money, and, perhaps, your pleasant or persuasive manner with people.

To be sure that you're on track, grade each cover letter with the following scoring sheet.

RedHot Cover Letter Checklist

A point value appears below each box. Most items are valued at 10 points; three items are so important to your success that they're worth 20 points on the RedHot range of high-powered persuasion.

The highest total you can reach is 300 points, including 20 points applying only to electronic letters (and not everyone will prepare an electronic letter).

If you're distributing your letter electronically, you need a full 300 points to be considered a hot-wired contender. Otherwise, if your letter points total 280, you've written a RedHot sensation!

Focus

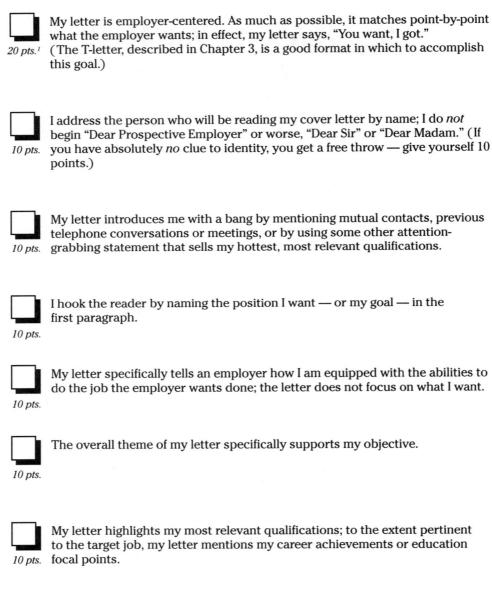

☐ My letter is employer-centered. As much as possible, it matches point-by-point
what the employer wants; in effect, my letter says, "You want, I got."
20 pts.[1] (The T-letter, described in Chapter 3, is a good format in which to accomplish
this goal.)

☐ I address the person who will be reading my cover letter by name; I do *not*
begin "Dear Prospective Employer" or worse, "Dear Sir" or "Dear Madam." (If
10 pts. you have absolutely *no* clue to identity, you get a free throw — give yourself 10
points.)

☐ My letter introduces me with a bang by mentioning mutual contacts, previous
telephone conversations or meetings, or by using some other attention-
10 pts. grabbing statement that sells my hottest, most relevant qualifications.

☐ I hook the reader by naming the position I want — or my goal — in the
first paragraph.
10 pts.

☐ My letter specifically tells an employer how I am equipped with the abilities to
do the job the employer wants done; the letter does not focus on what I want.
10 pts.

☐ The overall theme of my letter specifically supports my objective.
10 pts.

☐ My letter highlights my most relevant qualifications; to the extent pertinent
to the target job, my letter mentions my career achievements or education
10 pts. focal points.

Achievements and Skills

☐ My letter speaks of skills, not just responsibilities.

10 pts.

☐ My letter speaks of skills, not just responsibilities.*

10 pts.

☐ My letter speaks of skills, not just responsibilities.*

10 pts.

☐ For the most important skills, I cite at least one achievement; I measure achievements with real numbers, percentages, or dollar amounts to *10 pts.* establish credibility.

Length

☐ For cover letters attached to resumes, my letter is concise and limited to one page, consisting of three to six short paragraphs; for targeted letters replacing *10 pts.* resumes, my letter is limited to two, certainly no more than three, pages.

☐ I have avoided repeating the same words and phrases in my letter that appear on my resume.

10 pts.

---

* This point is so important, it bears repeating. Check once, check twice, then check again.

Contents

☐ I use powerful, selling words to give my letter that salsa bite.

10 pts.

☐ My statements illustrate specific product, company, and industry knowledge — they impress by suggesting that I did my homework.

10 pts.

☐ My letter contains KeyWords (nouns) that can be sought and retrieved by job computers.

10 pts.

☐ I translate acronyms, technical jargon, or military lingo into plain English, as necessary.

10 pts.

☐ I have not shot myself in the foot by mentioning negative or special issues — if I do mention such an issue, I have presented it in a savvy way.

10 pts.

☐ I have noted my education and training as it relates to my job target.

10 pts.

☐ I have closed my letter by suggesting an interview and by saying I will call at a given time.

10 pts.

☐ My letter uses enough (but not too much) industry-specific jargon, establishing my familiarity with the career field.

10 pts.

Layout

☐ I use the same 8.5- x 11-inch white or eggshell paper for my cover letter as I do for my resume. (Scanners accept other sized paper, such as Monarch, but the operator must stop and reset the scanner. This extra step often causes cover letters to be thrown away.) My letter, resume, and envelope are the same type of paper.

10 pts.

☐ The layout is open: minimum 1" margins — 1.25" or 1.5" margins are better; my letter looks visually appealing

10 pts.

☐ My cover letter uses familiar, scannable typefaces; it is word processed and laser printed (not typewritten or handwritten, which makes me look old-fashioned).

20 pts.[2]

☐ No handwriting is present on printed letterhead to correct an address or telephone number.

10 pts.

Proofreading

☐ My letter has no typos.

20 pts.[3]

☐ My letter has a return address and full contact information. If a resume is included, enough postage is on the parcel that the employer does not have to pay postage due, or I do not have to remail the entire package.

10 pts.

Comments

[1] 20 points for accenting employer's needs, showing how you are a point-by-point match for the job.

[2] 20 points for conforming to computer technology; letters that do not conform are left by the wayside because a job computer can't read them. Cover letters are considered a useful part of the applicant's file even in companies where cover letters are scanned into computers and not read by human eyes until a job match is made.

[3] 20 points for clean copy. Typos may make cover letter readers uneasy — if you're careless enough to misspell your application letter, what else will you be careless about?

Part IV
A Collection of
RedHot Cover Letters

The 5th Wave   By Rich Tennant

"Yes, Mr. Van Gogh, now that I have your
ear, so to speak, let me thank you for
that enticing cover letter."

In this part . . .

Some people are so gifted that they can sit down and assemble a bicycle without so much as looking at the instructions. The exceptionally gifted don't even end up with leftover nuts and bolts. Most of us, though, need to look at the blueprint to get a handle on how all the pieces fit together to make a solid bike.

Cover letters aren't much different. This book gives you the important details of putting together a RedHot cover letter. But what about some examples to drive the point home? These chapters show you a number of RedHot cover letters, complete with pointers on what makes them a good bet. Take some time to look over these letters. Then combine the points that work best with your achievements, skills, and goals.

Chapter 11

RedHot Responding Letters

- -

- -

*Y*ou see an ad. Your friend tells you about an opening in her company. These RedHot cover letters show ways you can respond to a variety of job opportunities and situations in which you may find yourself. You have lots of options. But the main point is to convince the reader that the job can't be filled before you have an interview.

Read through these samples. The names and identifying features have been changed, but the ideas remain the same. You'll also see some letters that help with tricky issues like rejecting a job offer, composing a recommendation, and throwing your cover letter to the winds of employers in a one-size-fits-almost-all broadcast approach. I added notes to help you see what makes these cover letters RedHot. Use these models to trigger ideas for your own RedHot responding letter, and start responding.

**Resume Letter
Social Worker**

KEVIN A. MIRAMONTES, SOCIAL WORKER
EAST COAST COLLEGE, 123-G ELEANOR HALL, BANGOR, MAINE 45678 (111) 213-1415
E-MAIL: MONTES@ECC.EDU

April 23, 199X   RE: HOME PARENTING SUPPORT JOB # HPS 432

MS. KATARINA M. SWARTZ, HUMAN RESOURCES MANAGER
AREA HOSPITALS INC.
NORFOLK NAVY BASE
1234 AVENIDA SALUD
NORFOLK, VIRGINIA 56789

DEAR MS. SWARTZ:

From my own childhood, I can remember the day I realized my parents (my father, a 20-year Navy man, my mother, a tough survivor of three children and 5 relocations) didn't have all the answers. Since then, I have pursued a life ambition to provide the kind of caring support and feedback military families like my own need. I can remember the graying family housing and the ever-present sadness surrounding Norfolk Navy Base. I am glad I can change that sadness —— the base needs good people who know how to sensitively, actively help its families.

Your opening for **home parenting support and crisis intervention services** caught my attention because it not only fits my background and academic concentration perfectly, but Norfolk is where Mom and Dad retired, and I will be returning there after I graduate with a Master of Arts in social work on May 21st. At the East Coast College, I have concentrated on precisely the areas your position requires experience in, including:

- **Child/spousal abuse prevention, reporting laws, knowledge of military family dynamics, crisis intervention, multi-lingual counseling (Spanish & English) and advocacy.**
- While completing my Master of Arts degree, I have been involved with an internship program off-campus, studying child abuse and **prevention in dual-parent English- and Spanish-speaking families.**
- In the last year of my baccalaureate study, I assisted the famous sociologist, Dr. Mariah D. Hersch, in researching **the dynamics of violence in military families** for a book that was published last year.

As you will see in my resume, I have both academic and clinical experience in home parenting support and in military family dynamics. My personal background has also well prepared me to empower individuals and prevent abuse, providing support that military families so desperately need. As dedication requires, I will work any hours necessary to make a difference in the lives of parents and children at Norfolk Navy Base. I will contact you next week to discuss the opening with you.

Sincerely yours,

Kevin A. Miramontes

Enclosure: Resume

A lengthy but irresistible letter.

**Resume Letter
Purchasing Agent**

SHAWN FULTON

495 Pembrooke | Chicago, Illinois 67777 | (708) 555-1212

June 1, 199X

Mr. Aaron Langdon
Human Resources Manager
Bentley Corporation
PO Box 123
San Diego, California 92101

**RE: Purchasing Agent
Ad: San Diego Union
May 26, 199X**

> Fulton's last job was "project manager," not "purchasing agent." Purchasing responsibilities clearly identified.

Dear Mr. Langdon:

My broad management experience in the fields of purchasing, logistics, distribution, and materials are an excellent match for the needs described in your advertisement.

Outlined below are some recent accomplishments exemplifying my additional capabilities in planning and budgeting as a project manager with purchasing responsibilities. This list serves as an illustration of the potential contributions that I can make to the Bentley Corporation:

> Ad called for salary history and references. Fulton asks for "mutual interest" before revealing salary requirements; references should not be overused.

* Saved $1.35 million and reduced overhead by 40% via a consolidated corporate air express services program for more than 1300 sites.

* Developed and implemented automated processing of over 25,000 purchase requisitions.

* Negotiated a design-build function for $13.8 million, 850-site, branch bank standards program, encompassing new merchandising fixtures and site refurbishings.

Once a mutual interest has been established, I will be pleased to discuss salary and references. For a beautiful spot such as San Diego, relocation costs are negotiable. I will contact you in the next week to discuss a convenient time to further explore how my skills and professional background will put my winter coat in storage and me on the road to San Diego.

Sincerely,

Shawn Fulton

Enclosure: Resume

> Usually it's best not to give away benefits like relocation costs up front. But when labor market for a position is strong, relocation costs are likely to keep Fulton from becoming a candidate. Fulton anticipated an objection and neutralizes it in advance.

**Resume Letter
Hotel Manager**

Patrick Howard Paul
345 Flower Street
Millsville, Arizona 75674
(555) 431-7890
E-mail: phpaul@prodigy.com

October 1, 199X

**RE: Your advertisement.
for a Night Manager
at the Millsville
Best Hotels**

Mr. David R. King
Vice President Operations
Best Hotels
4515 Sand Street.
Scottsdale, Arizona 75672

Dear Mr. King:

After working as a morning lark for a while, I'm ready to revert to my true nightingale status. I want that night manager's job!

As my resume indicates, I have worked as a front desk clerk at Motels In-The-Sand for two years. Having filled in for the night manager's days off for the last six months, I know how important it is to combine **solid accounting skills** with **good judgment**. I also know the pace can vary from slow to hectic with multiple crises needing attention in a single evening. I function well in chaos.

Now that I have tested the waters of this position, I want to jump in and perform the job full time. Where better to do that than at Best Hotels? I have read your annual report and know that your motto of "Service Day and Night" is a key to your success. I want to deliver that service as the Night Manager in Millsville.

My expertise in technology and management is at your disposal. I am confident that when we meet and further discuss your company's goals and my qualifications, you will agree that we are a match. I will call Thursday to schedule an appointment.

Sincerely,

Patrick H. Paul

Paul does his homework and reads the annual report. You can find this for public companies in the library.

Enclosure: Resume

**Resume Letter
Dietitian**

Namay N. Lee
12345 Whiskey River Road
Lexington, Kentucky 65329
(606) 555-1695

TWJ, Code D-U   RE: Dietitian Position:
P.O. Box 230013   University of Kentucky,
Lexington, Kentucky 65329-0001   Career Center Job Posting

May 3, 199X

Good Morning: ◄

> Good Morning is one way
> to avoid saying Dear Sir
> on a blind box ad.

Can you remember what you ate yesterday? My guess is somewhere along the line you ate lactose, milkfat, soy lecithin, corn syrup, partially hydrogenated soybean oil, cocoa powder, soy protein -- the dietitian's impression of a candy bar -- but what about vitamins A, B, C, D, E, and even K? I'll show you how to get tasty, proper nutrition -- without the candy bars! I'd like first, though, to tell you how I learned how.

To receive my Registered Dietitian Certificate (1/5/9X), I accepted an internship at Kentucky State Hospital, here in Lexington. Two years and 2,088 caring, working hours later, I have my certificate, and one extensive, vitamin, calcium, and protein-packed background in:

* nutritional counseling of: * planning menus
        pregnant women
        infants & children   * teaching nutrition classes

As part of a satellite outreach program funded by the hospital, I also provided community maternal-health care in the rural areas outskirting Lexington, developing skill in counseling mothers-to-be toward healthier, happier lives and children.

As you will see in the attached resume, your opening in ABC's new Women, Infants & Children program sparked my interest as a rare and timely match between my experience and ABC's recruitment interests. Please feel free to contact me anytime.

Healthfully yours,

Namay Lee

P.S.:   Vitamins A, B, C, D, E, and K appear in my dietary plan for mothers-to-be, which I would love to discuss with you in person.

Enclosure: Resume

**Resume Letter
Dental Hygienist**

Barbara Ann Timothy
4683 Pannee Road
Addison, TX 75240
(214) 555-3695

April 2, 199X

**Re: Dental Hygienist
with Periodontist Experience**

Donald Payne, DDS
2176 Belt Road
Richardson, TX 75263

Dear Dr. Payne:

Sparked by your need for a dental hygienist with periodontic experience, as posted in the *Texas Dental Monthly* on March 30, I can relieve your stress of finding the ideal person to fill the job. Beyond my demonstrated **technical abilities**, my qualifications most beneficial to your practice include

- Associate Degree in Dental Hygiene, Taper Medical Center, Fort Worth, TX
- 7 years' experience in periodontist practice
- Patient education: benefits of good oral hygiene, periodontal conditions, proper cleaning and care
- Hygienist education: patient care, cleaning, x-ray, and periodontist procedures
- Preparation of clinical and laboratory diagnostic tests for dentist
- Ability to recognize dental decay and gum disease
- Spanish fluency

Based upon these career highlights and those detailed in my enclosed resume, you will notice that I fit the bill as *the* prime candidate for your opening. I would be delighted to speak with you further about the match between my qualifications and the needs of your practice. I will contact you next week to set up an appointment.

Sincerely,

Barbara Timothy

A letter impressive in its simplicity.

Enc: Resume

**Resume Letter
Customer Service Representative**

KATELYN DICKERSON
48 Hillborough Drive
Washington, DC 02006
(555) 555-1212
E-Mail: kson@prodigy.com

June 23, 199X

Mr. Gerald Hail
Customer Service Supervisor
Big Bee Brands   **RE: CUSTOMER SERVICE REPRESENTATIVE**
1515 Fashion Square
Washington, DC 04321

> Dickerson's research shows this company has a serious personnel problem. She targets the reader by explaining how she will solve the problem.

Dear Mr. Hail:

Are you tired of your search for the one employee who can consistently get the job done? Are you weary of trying to find an associate who is self-motivated and self-directed so you need not stand over that person cracking a whip? I can help!

I am long on effort and enthusiasm...
        but short on procrastination and 30- minute "coffee breaks."

> Respond to requirements listed in job posting.

I achieve my goals at the end of the day, not the end of the week.

I am long on cooperation and a positive, friendly, productive atmosphere...
        but short on "finger-pointing" and cheap gossip.
                I am strong on interpersonal and communication skills.

I am long on customer satisfaction and exemplary service...
        but short on putting telephone customers on hold.
                *In my current position, I have a proven track record of
                98% "excellent" in customer satisfaction surveys.*

Mr. Hail, I'd love to have the opportunity to put my energy, drive, and determination to work for Big Bee Brands. May I further discuss your requirements during a personal meeting with you or one of your representatives? I understand the position advertised in the most recent copy of the Fashion Journal will be available August 1st. I am ready, willing and, as the enclosed resume shows, *more than able!*

Sincerely yours,

Katelyn Dickerson

> Leads reader to resume by hinting at impressive content.

Enclosure: Resume

Drake Fraser

1234 Pearl Street , Colleyville, TX 92120   **(123) 456-7891**

August 7, 199X

Ms. Marion Carver
Staffing Specialist
General Toys   **RE: Marketing Research Position**
12 Gallery Road
Irving, TX 75264

Dear Ms. Carver:

An opportunity to work for a company that creates toys! And better yet, toys that
combine creativity, education and, especially, fun. Life doesn't get much better.
For that reason, and because of my marketing experience for the past 15 years,
I would be thrilled at the chance to work for General Toys.

As Rosa Reyes, your administrative assistant, requested during our telephone
conversation today, I outline the requirements you are seeking as they align with
my skills.

Generating reports and market analysis ...
> **I have been in charge of all market analysis with my current
> company. Reports are based on basic demographic data and SIC
> codes.**

Making presentations and discussing marketing strategies ...
> **I currently organize and present 60% of my company's
> analysis and planning workshops. In addition, I present our most
> recent data at board meetings; generate presentations,
> graphs, pie charts, flip charts, and videos; and select guest
> speakers.**

Supervisory and management experience ...
> **I have been supervising a staff of up to three associates for the past
> eight years. My ratings as manager are consistently high.**

Even if I don't ever get to play with the merchandise at General Toys, I would
enjoy the opportunity to market them. When you believe in your product, work is
play! I will call you again next week.

Sincerely,

DRAKE FRASER

Enclosure: Resume

> Enthusiasm sells!
> Hard-hitting points are
> NOT the same ones that
> are on Fraser's resume.

Catherine Hill McAndrew
123 West Shore Lane
Small Town, NJ 12345
(201) 555-1212

July 15, 199X

RE: Mortgage Loan Officer

Ms. Marion Smith
Human Resource Manager
Big Money Mortgage
9 Central Park Street
New York, NY 14785

Dear Ms. Smith:

Tom Banks at your new district office in Newark, New Jersey, tells me that you're in the market for a Loan Officer, an exciting opportunity that I simply can't pass up.

My resume defines my skills in **marketing** and **operations.** In opening a new office in a state with unique lending guidelines and regulations, I believe both aspects of my past experience can benefit your company. For example:

> - **I can build and maintain a client base from ground zero.**
> - **I have an extensive contact-base in the Tri-State area with high profile clientele in New Jersey and New York.**
> - **I have experience as an operations manager with several major mortgage companies on the East Coast.**

Qualities that may not be readily apparent from my resume include being a person who embraces the ideas of respect and candor. I bring **integrity**, **intelligence**, and **energy** along with my diverse background and abilities to the position.

My exceptional **interpersonal** and **communication skills** will be key to the development of this office. As a seasoned veteran in the field, I recognize the need to clearly communicate to fellow employees and clientele the many intricacies of the mortgage industry.

Thank you for taking the time out of your demanding schedule to review my resume. I will call you on Tuesday morning to arrange an appointment to meet with you to discuss specifically what I can offer to Big Money Management.

Sincerely yours,

Catherine McAndrew

Enclosure: resume

> McAndrew will make her telephone call half an hour before normal work hours — and keep calling until she reaches Smith.

Dylan Hasselhoff, Web Page Designer

Juliet Plaza, 12 Ave della Arte
Verona, 3344556 Italy
Telephone: 67-78-89-91
Internet URL: www.tod.com
E-mail: dhassl@aol.com

January 28, 199X

Ms. Donna Aldeo, Art Director
Studio di Roma
Allegrito Boulevard, 654 Braggadocio Balustrade, Ste. K-38

Dear Ms. Aldeo:

Veronica Laertes recommended I contact you regarding a design position with Studio di Roma. As a result of studying and teaching courses in Web Page Design, your organization's extensive public visibility has made a great impression on me. I was especially energized when Veronica showed me your innovative designs for young, previously unknown companies, such as the now famous Pastaio Uno chain restaurant. I want a role in **Studio di Roma -- with me as a team member, the studio can be even stronger, tougher, and bigger.**

My experience at the University of Paris Art Department includes
- Three years' teaching computer illustration as part-time faculty
- Designing the University's Web Page
- Recipient of the Most Creative Web Design Techniques Award given by University of Paris Art Department -- selected from pool of 134 applicants

Did you know 40M Web Pages exist today, and it's an exploding arena? Such gazelles as Mama Maria Semolina Products, EuroTravel, and the recently publicized Bather's Choice began their first marketing successes on the World Wide Web.

My design expertise has prepared me to do big jobs for the smaller companies you service. I eagerly look forward to discussing how my diverse contributions and your successful designers can work toward stronger marketing with tougher technology to make Studio di Roma bigger profits and higher visibility. **I have some stronger, tougher, bigger ideas to show you!**

Sincerely yours,

Dylan Hasselhoff

Please check my Web Page to review my multimedia resume.

Use of boldface accentuates "selling motto" of letter.

Repeats selling motto to remind reader and exit with a bang!

**Resume Letter
Chemist**

Vincent Remady

11223 Farm Oaks Lane, Westminster, OR 55536
(555) 847-5555
e-mail: vremad@uofw.edu

April 12, 199X

Ms. Jane Winter
Unified Fibers & Plastics
Human Resources Director
6623 Concord Avenue
Westminster, OR 55536

**Re: Entry-Level Chemist: Job Hot Line,
University of Washington**

Dear Ms. Winter:

It would be a treasured opportunity to apply my **advanced education in chemistry**, to be completed in June, to the development of catalysts/materials in hydrocarbon processing and environmental applications for Unified.

My faculty advisor (Dr. Martin John) believes you will benefit from my previously acquired catalysis knowledge base. My educational research has spawned thorough familiarity with all aspects of catalysis structure and development. My qualifications include:

- **Thesis Focus:** selection, synthesis, and test of heterogeneous catalyst on a borazine/olefin system and utilizing this heterogeneous catalyst to insert carbon monoxide into a boron-hydrogen bond

- 5 years' research experience with three published articles

- Strong background in instrumental analysis and computer skills

- American Chemical Society's award for research *initiated* by a graduate student (selected from a pool of 256 graduate student applicants)

My **ability to work independently with thoroughness, motivation, and judgment** in combination with my education will provide valuable results for Unified. Expect a call from me within the week to arrange an appointment to further discuss your needs.

Sincerely yours,

Vincent Remady

Enclosure: Resume

Martin John, Remady's faculty advisor, knows Winter; so Remady drops John's name.

**Resume Letter
RF Engineer**

James M. Oldenstad

23476 Sparrow Lane
Framingham, MA 36952
(508) 555-3636
E-mail: jolden@dachey.daridu.org

June 14, 199X

Mr. Harvey Knott
Director, Employee Staffing
Veri Communications Inc.
36 Super Highway Road
Worcester, MA 36953

**Re: Senior RF Engineer Job Posting,
Veri WebSite**
Online Response 9-14-9X
Hard Copy Duplicate

Dear Mr. Knott:

Communications has come a long way from the tin can and string era; after 10 years as an engineer, it is terrific to still be excited about the hottest new developments. While visiting your WebSite last night to learn more about Veri Communications, I realized how advanced you are in the wireless arena.

The job listings show VCI's exponential growth! I want to contribute to that growth. When it comes to radio frequency technologies, I have:

- led a team of design engineers, technicians, and technical support staff in the design and development of digital multiplexers, analog telemetry, and high resolution video fiber optic communication products and equipment

- CATV projects management and engineering design competence

- experience with TOUCHSTONE, EAGLEWARE, and SPICE design tools

- over 12 years' diverse and progressive engineering management experience, with 4 of those years operating in Total Quality Management environments

If you want a skilled and enthusiastic communicator, I'm your man! I'll call on Wednesday for an appointment that fits your timetable.

Sincerely,

James M. Oldenstad

Enclosed: Resume

**Resume Letter
Speech-Language Pathologist**

Marisa Tomlinger
11 Park Street, Alfred, New York 14802
(201)555-1212   E-mail: ger@worldnet.att.com

E-mail address set apart
so computer can scan it.

September 13, 199X

Ms. Judith Ann Parson, Director
New York Rehabilitation Center
P.O. Box 45677
New York, New York 10128   RE: Speech-Language Pathologist position

*Knowing is not enough,
we must apply.
Willing is not enough,
we must do.*
-Goethe

The quote is a nice touch.

Dear Ms. Parson:

Having been a Speech-Language Pathologist for nearly **10 years**, and having spent most of that time **working with children who have severe speech and learning differences**, I have learned to live by this concept. With this in mind, I hope you will seriously consider me for the position advertised in the Sunday *New York Times.*

I have an extensive experience base in the New York area that will especially contribute to the growth of New York Rehabilitation Center. My concentrations include **children's speech therapy, speech analysis for all ages, adult speech therapy, and phonetics instruction.** My written and oral proficiency in Spanish and Italian will enable me to extend my services to a broad community.

I look forward to the opportunity of meeting you to discuss my background in further detail, since this letter only touches on the highlights of my career. I will contact you next week to do so. Thank you for your consideration.

Sincerely,

Marisa Tomlinger

Enclosure: Resume

Resume Letter
Compensation Manager

Jeffrey T. Donaldson
209 Hilltop Lane
Ridgewood, NJ 07825
(201) 555-7623

June 12, 199X

Mr. Ronald Redfinger
Senior Vice President, Human Resources
BITES Inc.
635 Colum Road
Morristown, NJ 07962

Re: Posting for Compensation Manager:
Job Bulletin Board, Conference of
Human Resource Professionals

Dear Mr. Redfinger:

How does an opportunity to lead BITES' compensation staff sound to me? Like a sound opportunity!

Helping fulfill CEO Mary Twists's goal of achieving higher productivity and operating margins is just the assignment I've been looking for.

As an asset to BITES Inc., my qualifications extend far beyond my focus in management compensation, to include research, public speaking, and written communication skills used to enhance productivity, quality, and value among employees and clients. My contributions to BITES will include

- Benchmarking and updating of pay for performance strategies and measures, in conjunction with other members of the Productivity & Quality Center based throughout the BITES organization

- Development of reward and recognition programs that reinforce economic value creation, as well as strategic gains in customer satisfaction, internal processes, and innovation -- the drivers of future financial performance

- Continuous year-to-year improvement in the ways that the overall pay system is communicated, resulting in clear signals -- to employees, customers, and shareholders -- of just what performance is expected and rewarded

As an expert resource to your business groups and divisions, I will **visualize and implement continuing excellence** to insure BITES remains on top of its corporate competitors. I will call on Thursday for an appointment to discuss your staffing needs.

Sincerely,

Jeffrey T. Donaldson

Enclosed: Resume

**Resume Letter
Production Technical Support**

Brian Russell
5701 Kentwood Place, Grand Rapids, MI 49504
(616) 555-1212

May 24, 199X

Mr. Richard Taylor, Employment Director
Precision Operation Company
P.O. Box 3333
Detroit, MI 49508   **RE: Production Technical Support**

Dear Mr. Taylor:

A wise man once said, "Never turn down the opportunity to solve a problem ... it is the process by which we solve that problem that we learn the most." That "wise man" was my father. I guess that explains why I look at technical support and troubleshooting as an opportunity. Someday, with all the problems I have solved in my nine years in technical support, I hope to be a very wise man indeed!

In listening to your job hot line advertisement, I couldn't help but notice that an excellent match exists between your needs and my experience, which includes:

*   More than **5 years' experience in planning, scheduling, tracking, and supervising a comprehensive, corrective, and preventative maintenance program** involving a wide range of power generation, distribution, and control equipment.

*   More than **7 years' experience in troubleshooting and repairing** 110, 220, 440, and 4160 VAC and 250 VDC electrical systems and equipment ranging from large motors and generators to portable electrical tools such as drills and saws.

*   Proficiency with **IBM-compatible personal computers and Windows-based software.**

I'll call on Tuesday to see when we can meet. I look forward to the opportunity to assist in solving your company's most challenging problems!

Sincerely,

Brian Russell

Interesting opening, but not pompous.

Enclosure: Resume

Nelson R. Harbor
12 Ave Sausser, Parque du Bon, Panache, France, 3456798
Telephone: (01)-11-11-31
E-mail: Harb@comp.com

1/2/9X

Mr. Liam Nielsenn
Recruitment/Retention Specialist   **Re: Case Manager Position**
Champagne Medical Centre
123 Ave du Monde, Champagne, France 3344567

Dear Mr. Nielsenn:

For the past eight years, I have worked in various positions at the Panache Sanitorium, including **Charge RN (two years), ICU (two years), and home health (six years).** As you will notice in my enclosed resume, many of my positions have involved numerous responsibilities above and beyond the standard job description.

Your recruitment advertisement requests that applicants possess management experience in

> *open heart cases, amputee medicine, head trauma, stroke trauma, pediatric rehabilitation, spinal cord injury, and infection control.*

I have managed teams of more than 10 nurses in:

> **open heart cases, amputee, nerve, burn, head, stroke and neck trauma cases, pediatric rehabilitation, spinal cord injury and surgery cases, and infection control.**

Such a background aptly prepared me for your case manager position.

My experience helped me adapt to all kinds of typical hospital situations, including failing life support equipment, understaffing, staff authorization, utilization revision and discharge issues, and team management. I have been **licensed in France for eight years, and I completed my CRRN Credential.** As my resume shows, my experience is well suited to the responsibilities of a case manager at a larger institution. I look forward to discussing the position further with you, and will contact you next week.

Sincerely,

Nelson R. Harbor

Without complaining about his job at Panache Sanitorium, Harbor subtly clarifies his interest in changing jobs.

Enclosure: Resume

In quoting the help-wanted ad, and then presenting his experience in the same layout (indented with the quote in italics, his experience in boldface), Harbor makes an undeniable visual and mental parallel between the employer's needs and his abilities.

**T-Letter
Associate Executive Director**

Charles DeWitt
105 Chaucer Street
Golden, CO 80301
(303) 555-1212

June 27, 199X

Ms. Sarah McMillan
Executive Director
American Purchasing Management, Inc.
3607 Jayton Road
Washington, DC 20203

**Re: Association Management
Job Posting E-Span
June 26, 199X**

Dear Ms. McMillan:

After speaking with membership director Mary Milton about your job requirements, I am thrilled to discover an exceptionally compatible match between your needs and my skills. **In addition to association management experience**, described on my resume, I have worked in the purchasing management field. A synopsis of my purchasing background:

Your needs:

* Four-year degree

* Interfacing and materials management

* Negotiating skills

* Supervisory experience

My qualifications:

* Bachelor of Science in Business/Economics, Master of Science in Business Management, and five years' experience with Purchasing and Materials Management

* Comprehensive management of materials for facilities and engineering services

* Success in negotiating cost-plus pricing strategies for goods and services

* Analytical, negotiation, communication, and leadership skills

I seem to have exactly the background you need to support your leadership. I will call to check on the progress of your search for an Associate Executive Director next week.

Sincerely yours,

Charles DeWitt

Enclosure: Resume

T-Letter
Accounting/Assistant Controller

LAWRENCE J. KUHN
19 CHARLES LANE, SCHAMBURG, IL 60191
(555) 555-1212

Mr. Josh Thomas, President
Thomas and Associates
1300 N. Collingham Drive
Chicago, IL 61092

August 24, 199X
RE: Your Accounting/Assistant Controller Position
(Referred by Doug Orr, VP)

Dear Mr. Thomas:

Refers to a mutual contact.

As a management professional with demonstrated success in maintaining budgets and business reporting, I am seeking a new career challenge as an assistant controller. Doug Orr was confident we could mutually benefit from my expertise.

In speaking with Doug, a former colleague at Olds and Young, about the job requirements of your position, I discovered a compatible match between your needs and my experiences. They include

Your Needs:	*My Offerings:*
* Four-year degree	* BS in accounting
* CPA credential	* CPA + continued training
* Reporting experience	* Compiled data for weekly, monthly, quarterly, and annual reports and inventory valuations; created balance sheet and cash flow analysis
* Computer proficiency	* PC Lotus, WordPerfect, Excel, and General Ledger Applications
* Accounting systems implementation	* 100% increase in production through creation of streamlined systems and reporting

Offer me the chance to increase your productivity, and we will both benefit from our ability to implement positive change. I will call early next week to discuss how we can explore this possibility further. Thank you.

Sincerely,

Lawrence J. Kuhn

Ends with a friendly, constructive tone.

**T-Letter
Senior Systems Engineer**

CHRISTOPHER PURCEL
333 Green Park, New Brunswick Borough 99317, London, U.K. (11)-22-33-44

July 5, 199X

Hannah Hoffman, Engineering Resources, Tech House
654 Woodredge Lane
Hillsborough, 44567, London, United Kingdom

*It's no use saying, "We are doing our best." You have got to succeed in doing what is
necessary.*   --Winston Churchill

I fervently agree, Ms. Hoffman, with Churchill's no-nonsense approach. In fact, in today's
high tech world, his words have even more relevance! Part of "doing what is necessary," as
you well know, includes hiring the right people to get the job done. I am the candidate who
can get the job done. Below is a list of qualifications required as specified in your July 2,
199X ad in the *Financial Times*, for **Sr. System Engineers**. As you can see, I do what is
necessary, and then some.

BACHELOR OF SCIENCE IN ENGINEERING ...

BS in Electrical Engineering, Queens University

EXPERIENCE WITH SATCOM SYSTEMS ...

18 years' experience as systems engineer. Lead Systems Engineer on
VSAT design analysis, and trade studies. Simulated, analyzed, and tested
network and terminal concepts. 68% improvements on all systems tested.

**PROFICIENCY IN PROVIDING PRESENTATIONS AND ADVANCING
BUSINESS ...**

13 years' assisting customers in defining system requirements; presented
technical material at customer meetings; wrote technical requirement
documents. Developed ability to translate technical subjects to nontechnical
individuals, resulting in 80% of prospects purchasing system.

For more details on the information listed, please see the enclosed resume. I will call your
office next week to discuss my qualifications more in depth.

Sincerely,

Christopher Purcel

Enclosure: Resume

> Using Hoffman's name in first line replaces customary salutation so quote has full impact.

**T-Letter
Electronics Engineer**

ELISABETH MARTIN
1355 State Street
New Haven, CT 02222
(555) 555-1212
E-mail: emartin@jfuribe.com

May 31, 199X

Mr. Bill Truesdale, Staffing Representative
Aerospace Technologies
17 Manhattan Avenue
New York City, NY 10022

CONFIDENTIAL

RE: Electronics Engineer

Martin marks her resume
Confidential hoping her
boss won't find out she's
looking around.

Dear Mr. Truesdale:

Mentions industry
competitor to
show field savvy.

Although I am currently employed by your primary competitor, I recognize that
Aerospace Technologies indisputably represents "the best" in the aerospace industry.
Therefore, I have been calling your job hot line for the past six months in search of just
the right position to match my diverse professional background. Yesterday, I found it!

YOU SEEK ...	AND I BRING ...
a Bachelor's Degree	**Bachelor of Science Degree** in Electronics/Engineering
5 years' engineering and management experience	5 years' experience as **Electronics Engineer and Supervisor**
technology development experience	**Technology development and implementation,** including radar, research equipment, and fuel systems

Of course, this abbreviated list represents only the experience that most directly
corresponded with your hot line, so I am also enclosing a resume. I am available to you
at your earliest convenience and look forward to discussing my background with you. I
will call next week in hopes that we can do so. Thank you.

Sincerely yours,

Elisabeth Martin

Enclosure: Resume

Martin has a master's degree in
engineering and also 7 years of
experience. She answers as the job
hot line listing requires. She assumes
the listing means at least a
bachelor's degree and at least 5
years' experience; otherwise she may
be rejected for being "overqualified."

Blind Ad Reply Letter Attorney

Rosa Vargas
P.O. Box 2632
El Paso, TX 79913
(505) 283-5555

June 23, 199X

P.O. Box 9980
Dayton, OH 67321

Re: Senior Counsel:
Your Advertisement
El Paso Law Monthly, June 199X

To Whom it May Concern:

Low-key, professional letter responds to a blind box ad

I currently serve as senior U.S. counsel to the largest law firm in Mexico, Rodriguez y Gonzalez Baz. My qualifications which parallel the requirements outlined for a position as in-house Senior Counsel include:

- 15 years' international law experience
- Juris Doctorate from University of California, Berkeley Law School
- Certified by the American Bar Association, California Bar, Texas Bar
- Fluent in Spanish
- Strong legal research and writing skills

In my capacity as senior counsel, my responsibilities include:

- Representation of major US-based multinational corporations with business connections in Mexico and other Latin American countries
- Organizing internal legal staff of 5
- Directing communication between inside and outside counsel to ensure effective business dealings
- Determining companies' compliance with US and Latin American laws, customs, and business practices

The requirement of multi-national involvement, particularly the Latin American division, matches my qualifications for this position. My exemplary international law and bilingual skills will provide definite benefits for your company. I enclose my curriculum vitae and references for your review. Although I am currently employed by a competitor, my demonstrated knowledge and dedication to productive international business relationships and passion for international law mark me as the ideal candidate to fill your opening. I will contact you Wednesday for an appointment.

Sincerely,

Rosa Vargas

Enc: CV

Vargas encloses references because the ad asked for them.

**Employment Service Letter
Environmental Engineer**

February 2, 199X

Beth Walton
123 Brick Road
Baton Rouge, LA
75038
(456) 978-1011

Mr. John Dodge, Partner
Dodge & Dodge Recruiters
Akron, OH 36252

A computer will trip over the graphic design at the top of this letter.

Dear Mr. Dodge:

My professional experience and educational background make me a strong candidate for the **Environmental Engineer** position for which you are conducting a search.

Highlights of reasons why I will be a great asset to your client:

- **Ten years' experience as an industrial environmentalist**

- **Master of Science degree in environmental engineering, cum laude, Ohio State University**

As you'll see in my enclosed resume, my additional stint in the aerospace industry gave me the opportunity to apply federal and state health and safety regulations in a range of manufacturing environments, with certification in:

- **Industrial/Environmental Hygiene**

- **Environmental Inspection & Design**

Your client needs people with as many talents as possible, who understand the environmental industry from more than one perspective. My professional experience in the aerospace industry plus my in-depth studies at Ohio State University will enable me to make crucial contributions. Feel free to contact my anytime -- I'll call you within a few days to discuss what I can do and how I plan to do it.

Sincerely,

Enclosure: Resume

Beth Walton

Targeted Letter Cybrarian

Harriet Powers
5850 Day Street
Oklahoma City, OK 32843

March 17, 199X

Mr. Albert Betti, CEO
Bakewell Financial Products Inc.
2635 New Street
Oklahoma City, OK 32843

RE: Your Online Career Center
posting: corporate cybrarian--
"Librarian of Cyberspace"

Call me at (777) 538-9900
E-Mail me at:
sunnyk@worldnet.att.com

Dear Mr. Betti:

Can I online-review patent holdings and trademarks? You bet I can! I start with Derwood World Patent Index and TrademarkLookUp. Or Assists, ALIO, and U.S. Patents TotalText. Recently, I checked for Bonda's patents without success, but a trademark search showed that Bonda Technologies Inc. registered "WithMe" on October 21, 199X.

Can I dig out the latest online investment analysts' reports? You bet I can! I start with InvestWorld, the major database of investment analysts' reports. Five reports were found that discussed Bakewell Financial Products. You enjoy a good reputation.

Can I uncover corporate structures? You bet I can! When you want to know who owns a company, what the company owns, or who its subsidiaries are, I mouse over to the online database for Company Affiliations to answer these questions. I found, for instance, that Bakewell has one subsidiary listed: Bakewell Financial Products Ltd.,in London.

I have formal librarian training and have worked part-time as an information broker for three years. Keeping a handle on the fast flying information a thriving company needs today is a challenge. I'm good at it! Is tomorrow too soon to talk?

Sincerely yours,

Harriet Powers

> Powers "proves" she can do the job with three smart examples followed by a "can do" affirmation for each. She has formal librarian training, but not a degree in librarianship. Because cybrarians — for public, school, or corporate libraries — are still rare, she can afford to hold the resume for the interview. This letter was hand delivered to the company receptionist.

**Targeted Letter
Computer Programmer**

Paula Smith
36 Home Avenue
Etobicore, Ontario M5P358
(416) 555-1676
E-mail: psmith@prodigy.com

January 13, 199X

Mr. Craig McCormick   **RE: Director Applications Development**
VP MIS
Health Care Centers Inc.
26 Bellflower Street   Smith is writing to a Vice President
Toronto, Ontario M5P355   Management Information Systems
                                and using a mutual business
                                acquaintance as the introduction.
Dear Mr. McCormick:

Bob Firth of HBE Computers told me of your desire to find a Director of Applications
Development -- he believes, as I do, that my qualifications are a perfect fit.

I am a Senior Manager of Application Development with experience managing the informational
needs of a Canadian company with over $100 million in annual revenues. As a key member of
the management team, I have directed the implementation of computer technology which has
reduced expenses by 20%. This application has been used in both Canada and the U.S. The
following is the tip of the iceberg when it comes to my accomplishments:

> *   Directed a $2.5 million corporate-wide UNIX development project;
>   the system is installed in 350+ sites around the globe.

> *   Established network criteria for marketing and operations divisions,
>   then directed implementation. The network has run error-free
>   for over 12 months.

My reputation is that of a solid, strategic thinker who digests complex information and builds
coherent, actionable structure from that information, and then proceeds to get the job done. I am
eager to meet with you to discuss your corporate objectives as well as the contributions I can
make as Director of Application Development. I will contact you in a few days to set up an
appointment that fits into your schedule. Bob Firth may call you about me this week.

Sincerely,

Paula Smith

Smith will make
sure that Firth
makes the call!

Smith wants to
go from a Senior
Manager to a
Director so she
leads with
something she
directed.

**Targeted Letter
Catering Manager**

JAMES T. LUMSDALE

888 West Clinton Drive, Phoenix, AZ 85020   (602) 555-1212

March 20, 1998

Mr. Stan Acres, Human Resources Manager
American Catering Corporation
126 Sun Street
Phoenix, AZ 85032   **RE: Catering Manager Position**

Dear Mr. Acres:

   While attending a friend's wedding last Saturday, one of your caterers, John Bolton, told me you were in the market for a catering manager. I was so enticed, I had to pursue this once-in-a-lifetime chance to join a catering company as classy as yours!

   I have been in the catering business for most of my life, so I couldn't help but notice the exceptional services American Catering offers! The food was superb @md not an easy task at an out-door wedding -- the staff was knowledgeable and took great pride in their work! I haven't witnessed a working environment like the one you have created in years, maybe never.

   I know American Catering can benefit from my conscientious service and performance in a high-volume setting. Here is a brief list of my achievements ...

   I have ...
   - **Nine years in banquet/special event catering, restaurant food services and operations.**
   - **Extensive presentation, menu coordination, and multiple course experience.**
   - **Won the Sun City Best Presentation Award for 199X.**
   - **Hired and trained many new employees, especially in the past 2 years.**
   - **Graduated from Cornell School of Restaurant Management.**

   I have lived in the Phoenix area and established clientele and business associations for the last 10 years. As you know, word of mouth is the best advertisement. Between your reputation and my contacts, I will be a profitable addition to American Catering.

   I can't stress enough the outstanding work American Catering provided for my friends. I would be honored to join such an impressive group! I was immediately comfortable with everyone -- and would fit right in. You will be hearing from me early next week so I can fill in the details of my background.

Sincerely,

James T. Lumsdale

> Lumsdale fortifies the accomplishments with award.

> Boldface and bullets call attention to top selling achievements.

Thomas Jamison
3636 Arbor Road
Willmington NC 67589
(632) 121-2289

October 7, 199X

Ms. Marjorie Walters
Engineering Technologies, Inc.   RE: Engineering Position
Manager Human Resources   Entry Level
44991 Harbor East
Willmington, NC 67589

Dear Ms. Walters:

The Career Fair to be held at NC State this November is an exciting opportunity for Engineering Technologies, Inc., to interview students interested in the entry level positions being advertised through the campus Placement Center. My job experience and high GPA (3.75) make me a prime candidate.

While finishing my degree evenings at NC State, I have acquired valuable career experience through full-time employment the last three years at Technological Applications Inc. (TAI), a small electronics contract manufacturer specializing in Surface Mount Technology.

Starting on the manufacturing line and working at various positions before being promoted to Supervisor, Test Operations, has given me hands-on understanding of the challenges of turning designs into working prototypes and full production units. TAI does not afford me the opportunity to work in the design arena; therefore, I am looking to move on once I receive my degree.

I believe my work experience combined with a practical classroom education at a respected university has given me valuable knowledge of today's industry, both academically and professionally. The references I can supply from TAI will also validate my dependability and creativity.

I would appreciate the opportunity to meet with your representative next month to discuss possible career opportunities with Engineering Technologies, Inc. I will call in a few days with the objective of setting up a meeting.

Sincerely,

Thomas Jamison

Jamison deals with why he will not stay with his current employer. The positive message is reinforced by bringing up the references.

Chapter 12

RedHot Initiating Letters

- -

In This Chapter

▶ Networking letters

▶ Internet-working letter

▶ Follow-up letters

▶ Recommendation letters

- -

C hapter 11 shows you a number of examples of responding letters. This chapter shows model letters where you take the initiative to write to ask others to help you with job leads, to ask employers to consider hiring you, to thank employers for interviews, to show appreciation to others who have lent a helping hand, and to accept or reject a job offer.

These are RedHot initiating letters. I've included my comments to point out things that make the letter RedHot. Take your cue from these letters and start initiating the leads and thank-yous that land you the ideal job.

Networking Letter: Competitor's Employees

Ari Trinh
Plano Research Department
101 Main Street, Plano, TX 75004
(213) 555-8888 days (213) 666-9999 eves

Ms. Maya McDonald
Cooper Systems Inc.
202 Lacan Circle
Columbia, OH 44122

April 8, 199X

RE: **Research Analyst position**

Dear Ms. McDonald,

Our mutual friend, **Cory Paine** recommended I write to you for assistance in my current job
search. I seek a position as an **operations systems analyst** or **statistical research analyst**. My
qualifications include:

— SIX YEARS' EXPERIENCE AS A STATISTICAL RESEARCH ANALYST

— MORE THAN 12 YEARS OF COLLEGE-LEVEL MATHEMATICS, STATISTICS

— EXTENSIVE KNOWLEDGE OF STATISTICAL RESEARCH

— PH.D. IN MATHEMATICS EDUCATION

— MASTER OF SCIENCE IN OPERATIONS RESEARCH

— BACHELOR OF SCIENCE IN MATHEMATICS AND STATISTICS

While my current position has been extremely rewarding, my financial needs require that I change
jobs for one that is more lucrative. I would appreciate any assistance you can give me in providing
job leads, contacts, or advice. You have worked in this field longer than I, and I would like to
learn from your greater experience. Be assured that I will return this favor in any way that I can.

Thank you,

Ari Trinh

Enclosure: 6 resumes

Trinh hopes his friend's name will
generate search assistance or at
least confidentiality for his search.

Networking Letter: Alumni

200 South First Street
Manhattan, KS 65042
(913) 776-6655
E-mail: fields@cts.com

February 5, 199X

Ms. Gaye Rivers
United Aerospace Co.
101 Summer Avenue
Springfield, AZ 90168

**RE: Aerospace Engineering position
sought by fellow alum of
Kansas State University**

Dear Ms. Rivers,

*When confronted with challenging problems,
knowing who to call upon for the answers is a valuable tool.*
Anonymous

As one alum to another, I'd like to feel that it's okay to call upon you for some answers to my
challenging first job search as an aerospace engineer.

My experience and qualifications include:
- Bachelor's in aerospace engineering expected May 199X
- Internship with American Signal Inc. for two summers (199X and 199X)
- Expect to graduate summa cum laude
- One-year senior design course
- Proficiency with CAD and panel method software
- Leadership and community service experience in Delta Delta Delta sorority
- Willing to relocate

If you know of positions open or people I should contact to best utilize my qualifications, please
let me know. In addition, I would love to hear how you got started and progressed as a successful
aerospace engineer. As a woman entering a predominantly male field, I can use whatever advice
you can offer.

I appreciate any time you can take to relate your advice or assistance. I'll call you in two weeks
for any ideas you may have.

Sincerely,

Marsha Fields

Marsha Fields

Enclosed: 3 Resumes

> Fields pulls out all the stops in asking
> an alumna of her gender and discipline
> to help her find a job. She got Rivers'
> name from her career center office,
> which worked through the alumni office.

Networking Letter: Friends and Family

Rolf Andersen   100 Ocean Drive, San Rafael, Florida 33300

(305) 444-4444
e-mail: anders@aol.com

Mr. Jack Robins   June 12, 199X
400 St. Louis Avenue
Ventura, NJ 07954   **RE: Sales and Marketing position**

Dear Jack,

Remember that political bet you lost to me last Christmas? Well, I've figured out how you can pay me back. Instead of dinner as we agreed, how about a job? Yeah, I know you can't give me a job, but I certainly could use some good leads, advice, or contacts.

Last month, my employer, International Gadgets, started downsizing, and I was surprised when the company laid off my entire support staff -- my personal secretary, my office manager, and my accountant! Suddenly, the "International Relations Department" became "Rolf Anderson." Picture me, secretaryless, struggling to search-and-plunk out all my correspondence! As you can imagine, I'd love to join a less self-destructive organization.

I have a pretty hot resume -- but it takes more than a piece of paper to get a job. In case you think of someone to refer me to, let me refresh you on my background:

* Managed international accounts for Dixon & Preece, Madison Avenue

* Sold for Florida Interstate Travel -- foreign and U.S. customer base

* M.A. Degree, 3.85 GPA, International Affairs, with a concentration in International Business and Economics, University of San Rafael, Florida

I've been looking for something in international business consulting, international marketing (as liaison with international subsidiaries/distributors), or international investment brokerage (specializing in Latin America) -- but I'm trainable, and I'd love to broaden my horizons; I welcome any advice.

So you have a choice: either pay the 30 bucks you owe me, or help me out in a much bigger way.

Thanks for everything Jack,

ROLF ANDERSEN

> *A good-natured spoof asking for help from a pal.*

P.S. I'm enclosing several copies of my resume in case you think of the perfect recipient.

Networking Letter Internet

Date: Mon, 18 Mar 199X 13:12:40
From: PixStix <rtk@roseshire.ac.uk>
RE: JobPlace <JOBPLACE@NEWS.JOBWEB.ORG>
Newsgroups: jobweb.jobplace
Subject: Placement year...

I am a second year student at Roseshire University in England reading
Geography. The third year of my degree course is termed a "placement"
year as I must find a job for at least 52 weeks in the period from July
199X to September 199X before continuing into the fourth and final year
of my degree.

I am looking for any companies or institutions worldwide (but especially
in Australia, New Zealand or around the Pacific Rim) that have a
temporary post such as this with a geographical/environmental interest. I
am willing to pay any travel expenses to reach the job. If you could help
me in any way I would be most grateful.

Thank you for your time,

Ryan King

rtk@roseshire.ac.uk

King posted worldwide on every job-related discussion group he
could find. Unfortunately for King, the JobPlace mailing list
(a feature of JobWeb, the World Wide Web site of the National
Association of Colleges and Employers) is not designed to help
people find jobs. Instead, it is a discussion group for professionals
in career counseling. King wasted everyone's time. LESSON TO
LEARN: Post a job appeal only where your message reaches a
target audience whose members have the power to say "yes."

Broadcast Letter

Ethan S. Nealen
11 Jamestown Road
Smithfield, RI 02917
(234) 567-8910

June 17, 199X

Ms. Gertrude Moser
Korris International
171 Random Lane
New Martinsville, WV 26155

Dear Ms. Moser:

Selling points
in bold letters.

While serving as a manufacturing **Director of Sales and Marketing**, I spearheaded the push for new products "out the door" -- doubling new product production within three years. As **Marketing Manager** for another manufacturer, I introduced exciting distributor incentive plans, changed product packaging and added fresh distribution channels -- **result: sales up 17% and profits 31%.**

My last company was sold, making me available for sales and marketing management with a key manufacturing organization such as Korris International.

As yet another example of the contribution I can make to Korris, I reduced the size of our packaging by 50% while improving box graphics. Direct results include:

"Enduser" is industry jargon for end user.

• Increased manufacturing turns
• Lower shipping weights/costs
• Lower box prices to endusers, increasing market share
• Improved distributor margins
• Higher sales and production volumes

My verifiable record gives me confidence that I can quickly contribute to your company's profitability by developing programs to capture real customer solutions -- not just another round of price discounting!

I would greatly appreciate the opportunity to discuss how my skills and experience can make a powerful and significant impact on your company's success. I will call your office in a few days to arrange an appointment.

Sincerely yours,

Ethan S. Nealen

Nealen has an e-mail address, but he does not list it. It is unlikely that Moser will pick up the telephone to call Nealen to say "Don't call, we're not hiring," but it is easy to use impersonal e-mail to tell him to bug off. Nealen is less likely to get the cold shoulder if the emplyer can only contact him by telephone.

Temp Reach-Out Letter

Sheveron S. Adams
12354 Beach Boulevard
Huntington Beach, California 98777

March 11, 199X

Mr. Brock Keifer
Manpower, Inc.
8989 Avenida Encinas
Huntington Beach, California 99860

Dear Mr. Keifer:

Can your clients use a top pick DRAFTER choice?

I have gained valuable drafting experience, and I'm looking for jobs where I can use my expertise to jump in and do great work from Day One. I am ambitious, self-disciplined, and work well under pressure without constant supervision. Previous employers (names on request) have called me "meticulous," "conscientious," and "dependable."

I believe my determination to achieve will prove to be an asset to your temporary services firm.

Thank you for your consideration. I look forward to talking with you soon.

Sincerely,

Sheveron S. Adams

(809) 234-9898
E-mail: ShevA@Prodigy.com

> Adams will call within the week to verify his marketing package (cover letter and resume) was received, and to ask about the frequency of drafting assignments.

Enclosure: Resume

> Note no mention is made of enclosing a resume in the body of the letter; that task is handled at the bottom of the letter.

Contract Job Letter

Juan Carlos Suarez
Villa de Rose, 20-4B
67895 Las Flores
Barcelona, 38671, Spain
Telephone: 11-22-33-44

January 7, 199X

Ms. Jillian Carson
Human Resources Manager
American Propulsion Inc.
PO Box 222222
New Castle, DE 19270
USA

> This powerful opening statement for a contract job assignment is carefully worded. It doesn't say Suarez has done this exact work, but refers to the type of "challenging project."

Dear Ms. Carson:

Your new Blazer contract -- the talk of the industry! -- sounds very interesting -- just the type of challenging project that I've spent the last six years doing.

That's why I seek a **project assignment** for a **senior aerospace engineering position** with American Propulsion Inc. My contractual obligations in Europe with Global Aerospace are coming to a close soon. Briefly, my background includes:

- Manufacturing process planning
- Quality engineering
- Procurement experience
- Project development
- Configuration engineering
- Multinational consortium coordinator
- NATO secret clearance
- European aerospace industry specialist
- Computer savvy

My attached resume describes my superior qualifications for top-of-the-line aerospace engineering projects. I will be in the United States **on the East Coast from January 20 to February 19.** I'll contact you when I arrive to explore your staffing requirements. I look forward to meeting you.

Sincerely yours,

Juan Carlos Suarez

> Suarez won't be ready to start a new assignment until May, but notice he doesn't mention that fact. The January 20 to February 19 trip is for scouting purposes only. If he does a good job of selling his qualifications, the employer will probably wait for him.

Summer Job

Marek Tellison
65 Torkle Drive
Highland Park, IL 66666
(619) 777-8888 (Until May 2)
(708) 232-8653 (After May 2)
April 12, 199X

Ms. Dionne Devereaux, Manager
Dolluloid Accounting Group   **RE: SUMMER INTERNSHIP 199X**
7175 Wacker Drive, 8th Floor
Chicago, IL 50026

Dear Ms. Devereaux:

Flash of personality balances numbers-
oriented accounting — suggesting a
serious but fun guy to have around.

"If you wish to reach the highest, begin at the lowest."
--Publius Syrus

I know my quoting Publius Syrus is a sign of youthful idealism @md that's me!
And I have the energy for hard work that goes with it.

Thank you for today's discussion of the summer internship opportunities present
at Dolluloid. I am glad that Peter Hare referred me to you. The situations we
discussed sound both challenging and exciting.

As mentioned, I will soon finish my junior year at San Diego State University as
an accounting major, and I will be home in Chicago until early September.

As you pointed out, San Diego State University has provided me with an excellent
background and foundation in both accounting and personal development. I have
completed the following courses:

Financial Accounting courses:
        -- Managerial Accounting
        -- Intermediate Accounting I and II
        -- Accounting Information Systems
        -- Income Tax
        -- Micro and Macro Economics
        -- Financial Markets.

I am proficient with PC and Macintosh software including Word, Windows,
Excel, Lotus 1-2-3, WordPerfect, Quicken, MacWrite, and AppleWorks.
                        (1 of 2)

Ms. Dionne Devereaux/Marek Tellison

As the President of the Alpha Pi Fraternity, I have continued to sharpen both my interpersonal skills and my leadership abilities. I am gaining valuable experience in leading, motivating, and organizing the combined efforts of more than 60 men. I have learned the importance of doing independent work in a timely and pressured environment as part of a greater team.

This understanding can be exemplified by our chapter's recent success in being chosen for the Grand Piano Award, presented to one of the three best chapters in the United States and Canada for 1993-1995.

I have also gained additional experience in interacting with school officials, advisors, and prominent community leaders.

I believe these skills will assist me in supporting your staff to strengthen client relationships, and enable me to perform as a contributing team member.

I was able to advance my business background with an internship at Moe, Hauk & Smith (San Diego) during the fall of 199X. With my soon to be awarded accounting degree, as well as my membership in the Student Accounting Association, I feel very secure about my accounting abilities as an entry-level employee of your company.

I look forward to further discussing a summer internship position with you. I am very excited about any opportunity that I might have to capitalize on my accounting background and assist your company's needs this summer. Thank you very much for your time and consideration.

Sincerely,

Marek Tellison

Enclosures: Resume, Transcript

Follow-Up to Meeting

4444 Milky Way Drive
Sun Beach, CA 90090
(900) 606-4004
E-mail: rayl@worldnet.att.com

June 21, 199X

Ms. Alex Sunni   RE: Associate Editor Position
Editor
Astronomical News Magazine
33 Nova Lane
Carlsbad, CA 92124

> Leight begins with a
> shared experience,
> much stronger than
> "Here's my resume."

Dear Ms. Sunni:

I truly enjoyed meeting you last Saturday at the Carlsbad Sundowner's Club. It's always refreshing to spend time with fellow senior star-gazers, and I want to thank you for sharing your amazing knowledge of black holes with me.

As you requested, I have enclosed my resume for your review. Your job opening for an associate editor sounds fascinating, and with my 30 years of experience in writing, research, and editorial work, I can bring a wealth of professional experience to this position. In addition, my education in astronomy and my years of gazing through telescopes invest me with a personal interest in the growth of your magazine.

I look forward to speaking with you soon so that we can discuss specifics of how I can contribute to your magazine.

Best Regards,

Ray F. Leight

Ray F. Leight

Enclosure: resume

Follow-Up To Telephone Call

999 Rocky Plaza
Mountain City, TX 76444
(765) 432-9876
E-mail: stone@worldnet.att.com

July 14, 199X

Mr. Juan Cedres, CEO   RE: GIS position
Map Attack
888 Boulder Street, Suite 8
Pebble Beach, TX 77665

Dear Mr. Cedres:

Thank you for taking the time to speak with me yesterday about the possibility of creating a position for a Geographic Information Systems Specialist. As you requested, I have enclosed a resume for your consideration.

As we agreed during our telephone conversation, Map Attack's expansion will depend upon innovative software. My knowledge of **AML**, a GIS programming language, and my recent education in **geography** and **computer science** enable me to create mapping software for commercial distribution as well as for company-wide distribution of easy-to-read plans and reports.

I welcome the chance for a personal meeting with you to discuss in more detail how I can help ease Map Attack's growing pains.

Sincerely,

Dustin Stone

Dustin Stone

Enclosure: resume

Thank You for Job Interview

Grant Wang
4590 Tinwood Circle
Roswell, NM 88202
(777) 316-9808
E-mail gwang@net.com

October 30, 199X

Mr. Jeffrey Hano
Staffing Specialist
Human Resources Center
Fountain Corporation
PO Box 46234
Medford, OR 44444

> Adding new information sets your thank-you letter apart
> from the Thanks-Aunt-Martha-for-the-socks variety.

Dear Mr. Hano:

Thank you for interviewing me yesterday for a **mechanical engineering position.**
You said you'll soon be routing my resume to several departmental managers. I'll
look forward to hearing from interested managers -- I believe I can show them
how I meet their needs for a high-performance mechanical engineer.

We were so occupied talking about my skills with hydraulic equipment and
precision machining that I am not certain I fully described my experience with
hydro-electric plant technology yesterday, but I note in today's newspaper that
Fountain expects to land a major contract to build a plant in a developing nation. I
enclose a summary of my hydro-electric plant experience with this letter and
would be happy to detail my experience with you or with the appropriate
departmental manager.

Many thanks. I hope we'll have much more to talk about soon.

Sincerely yours,

Grant Wang

Enclosure: Hydro-electric resume addendum

> Sending a resume addendum is not a good idea — separate papers slip though the cracks. But here,
> timing counts. A new contract means heavy new staffing efforts — lots of work. Hano will remember
> interviewing Wang just a couple of days ago and perhaps see a way to lighten his recruiting load.

Thank You for Job Interview

Edie M. Schustermann
12345 North Sunder Court
Dallas, Texas 75248
Home: (678) 910-1112
Message: (131) 415-1617
E-mail:ann.ddd@edu

March 18, 199X

Ms. Bethany Marsh, Marketing Director
World Wind Travel Gear, Inc.
444 Roving River Way
Fort Worth, Texas 56789

Dear Ms. Marsh:

I can hardly wait to work for you! I appreciate the time you spent interviewing me today for a **MARKETING TRAINEE POSITION**. I was excited to learn the position requires several annual trips to the Australian office. Although we only had time to discuss my education and work experience in detail, I wanted to remind you about my exposure to the Australian market.

During my undergraduate studies in international relations, I spent three informal summer months in Sydney drinking in *shrimp-on-the-barbie* culture. It was a great experience in bridging my US background with the way things are done Down Under. I made good friends with several advertising account executives at the *Ayers Rock News*, and I developed contacts with personnel at two major Bemberg travel agencies.

Please don't forget my Australian connection when you decide how to fill the ranks of World Wind Travel Gear's young adult marketing staff.

While we were talking, I realized how well my Australian-flavored background fits into your organization -- from the directions of your advertising campaigns to your target market. This job has my name on it!

Sincerely yours,

Edie M. Schustermann

Her GPA won't win awards so Schustermann compensates by emphasizing another selling point — the summer she spent bopping around Sydney. Always look for a way to compensate for a weakness.

Thank You for Job Interview

Maxwell Hong
123-D North Circle Drive, Toronto, Canada 44567
Telephone: 22-33-44-55
Internet URL HTTP:\\WWW.BUILDNET.FREELANCE\MAXHONG
E-mail: mhong@aol.com

September 7, 199X

Mr. Brent C. Nababy, Vice President
21st Century Developments
5555 Hassau Broadway
Toronto, Canada 44568

Dear Mr. Nababy:

Thank you for the opportunity to interview for a sub-contractor coordinator position. I was impressed with the warmth and efficiency of your offices and your genuine interest in acquainting me with your staff and company goals.

Opens with personable style and quick reminder of interview.

During our discussion, I told you about my background in sub-contractor coordinating. Although our conversation focused on hiring policies, top contacts, and scheduling strategies, I wanted to underscore our mutual priorities. The latest issue of *Building Issues* brings to my attention a priority we share: "Beating the competition's quality by miles."

Reviews salient points made during interview.

I have always strived to reach high quality results by using the most appropriate materials and by studying the quality of materials used by other companies. Among my favorite suppliers, you may recognize the following names: Namath Re-bar, Drywall By-the-Mile, and Lionel Fixtures.

Includes interests not fully covered in interview, uses company motto.

Such high standards have been so central in my work that I feel compelled to join such a demanding company as yours. Thanks again for the interview. I look forward to contacting you next week to check on the progress of your search.

Mentions contacts not included on resume.

Signs off with intent to follow-up.

Sincerely,

Max Hong

Thank You for Referral

222 Phantom Way
Ghost Town, CA 92126
(444) 123-1231

October 31, 199X

Ms. Susan Specter   RE: Referral to Paula Geist
Spirit Products, Inc.
333 Incorporeal Circle
Apparition, CA 92137

Dear Ms. Specter:

Your help with my job search has been out of this world! Thank you for all of your advice. Most specifically, thank you for referring me to Paula Geist at Geist, Deeman, and Hant.

I have left several voice-mail messages for Ms. Geist this week. Yesterday, her assistant informed me that Ms. Geist returned from a business trip three days ago, so I expect to hear from her soon.

I have enclosed a copy of my resume for your perusal. A million thanks in advance if you think of anyone else I should call. I hope you know how much I appreciate all of your kind assistance.

With sincerest gratitude,

Dorcas Wraith

Dorcas Wraith

Enclosure: Resume

> If Geist doesn't call Wraith, Specter may follow up, asking that Geist do so. Note subtle suggestion that Specter continue to refer Wraith to other potential employers.

Acceptance Letter

Brooke Lancaster
34567 Unity Square
Troy, MI 48098

February 15, 199X

Drew McCallister
Sales and Marketing
Walters and Sons Construction Firm
5577 Fairview Drive
Grand Rapids, MI 49503

> Lancaster writes more than an acceptance letter: He incorporates his understanding of conditions offered. While not legally binding, if a dispute occurs, Lancaster at least has some paperwork to confirm his understanding of the offer.

Dear Mr. McCallister:

I am pleased to accept your offer for the position of Assistant Supervisor of Sales and Marketing for Walters and Sons Construction at a starting salary of $3000 per month, plus reimbursement for relocation costs up to a maximum of $12,000. As we discussed, I will receive the standard benefits package, which includes health coverage and retirement contributions.

I am looking forward to extending my ideas and expertise into the sales and marketing division of your company. My extensive background in sales and marketing will allow me to get started immediately with minimal training. Within three weeks, as we predicted, I should know the company well enough to relieve you and Maria Espinoza of the bulk of the marketing and sales responsibilities so you can focus more intently on the regional expansion of Walters and Sons Construction.

As you are aware, I am currently securing my living situation to relocate to Grand Rapids. I expect to conclude this endeavor by mid-March, in which case I will be able to begin working by March 28, 1998. If this arrangement is inconvenient or you would like to present another option, please let me know. I will contact you by March 2 to cement final arrangements.

I am excited to join your team and thank you for the opportunity to participate in the growth and dynamism of Walters and Sons Construction.

Thankfully yours,

Brooke Lancaster
(718) 692-7777

Rejection Letter

Trevor Taylor
3456 Griffin Place #7
Rogers, AR 72757

January 7, 199X

Grant Focault
Human Resource Department
GreenTree Corporation
Rupert, ID 83350

> Note the grace with which Taylor turns down a job. Focault may be promoted to an even bigger newspaper and offer Taylor an even better job someday.

Dear Mr. Focault:

I would like to extend my thanks to you for offering me the position as **Features Editor** for the *Idaho Daily Times*. I feel fortunate to have had the opportunity to discuss this position with you.

I was quite impressed by you and your team at the paper. However, since we last talked, I have accepted another editorial position for a publisher in my area. Because of the location and my inability to relocate, I feel this position better suits my present needs.

Again, the opportunity to learn about your newspaper and its operations has been an enlightening experience. I am confident that your success will extend into future endeavors, and I am sorry that I cannot join your team at this time.

Best Regards,

Trevor Taylor

Recommendation Letter

March 15, 199X   **Re: Higher Education Faculty**

To Whom It May Concern:

Susan Reardon has been a valued associate and friend for over fifteen years. During that time I employed her as an editorial/research supervisor for two long periods. Currently she is working with me as a writer/consultant for a book I plan to publish in the next year.

I first met Susan when she was a senior in high school. Even then I considered her editorial skills to be superior in the field; she proved an invaluable resource for research and editorial knowledge. Since then, she has developed an enormous range of interests and talents, from calculus to art history, that can bring true diversity to her teaching objectives and perspective.

Susan has tremendous skills in writing and communication which can only help in reaching her students' interest. Her editorial work is consistently reliable, independent, and polished, attesting to her professionalism and dedication. In the past year she has undertaken a variety of projects which show talent, range, and creativity. These projects include an effort to combine her analytic and communicative skills by developing a series of children's mathematics books.

Susan possesses a genuine commitment to mathematics education encompassing the needs of elementary-age students, to whom her manuscript is targeted, as well as encompassing the needs of college students whom she has taught. In addition, she is passionate about bringing mathematics to those who are under-represented by the traditional profile of mathematicians. Her own educational experiences fostered a concern for the shortage of women and minorities in mathematics. Her passion for mathematics and commitment to teaching, combined with her superior communication skills and professionalism, make her well-suited to work toward the goals of the community college system as she is eager to do.

Susan is contagiously enthusiastic about her field and well-prepared to introduce new students to mathematical concepts with innovative and flexible teaching approaches. Susan will be an asset to any mathematics department. Please feel free to call me if you have any questions.

Sincerely,

Michele-Ann Lawrence

Michele-Ann Lawrence
(121) 672-1111

> This letter is placed in Reardon's credentials file at her university career center.

Part V
The Part of Tens

"I sent my cover letter over the Internet and got 3 responses in less than a week. Unfortunately they're from 3 different continents, none of which I live on."

In this part . . .

No Dummies book would be complete without the Part of Tens. This part sums up ten tips (more or less) for just about everything to help your job search succeed — working with recruiters, answering job ads, avoiding the salary question, handling negative references, and creating letters that even a computer can love. Read through this information to get you that final mile to the all-important job interview.

Chapter 13

Ten Tips to Buddy Up to Computers

● ●

In This Chapter

▶ Making your cover letter computer-friendly

● ●

*O*nline databases and electronic resume scanners are changing the way people find new jobs. A RedHot letter that wows human readers may be poison to computer scanning software. Here are ten tips to creating an electrifying, computer-scannable cover letter.

Avoid Underlining

Underlining for emphasis in your cover letter is not a wise decision. The lines can combine with the text above — creating a royal goof-up: Franklin becomes Eranklin, for instance. Leave a minimum of $1/4$ inch of space around all horizontal lines.

Use White or Off-White Paper

Using colored paper on your cover letter weakens the contrast between the text and paper. Very few computers have the ability to read text when the contrast is low. Save pale-colored paper for human readers; hew to straight black and white for the computer.

Avoid Script and Italics

Script and italics should not be used for the same reason you don't use underlining; both destroy text clarity as characters can run together. Newer software can read italics, but most of those in use can't. Always go with the lowest common denominator when dealing with the great diversity of technology in business.

Use Parentheses around Telephone Numbers

Whenever you list a telephone number, place the area code within parentheses; that's how computers identify telephone numbers.

Separate E-Mail Addresses

In your contact information, list your e-mail address if you have one. If you also have a URL (uniform resource locator) address on the Internet that includes a multimedia resume, list that, too. Separate an e-mail and URL address from your telephone number or fax number. You can put any two of these on the same line by placing one flush right and the other flush left (leaving plenty of white space between), or place them on separate lines. Otherwise a computer may jumble your contact information.

Use KeyWords

Just as in your resume, include KeyWords — nouns — in your cover letter. The job seekers with the most KeyWords, plus required experience, rise to the top of the candidate heap. Cover your bases by lacing your letter with career-specific KeyWords.

No Folds, No Staples

Send your letter in a full-size 8.5- x 11- inch envelope to avoid creases from folding. Use a paper clip to attach pages; not a staple. (Staples take extra time to pull out before feeding paper into the scanner.) Folds and holes impair the scanning software's ability to read the document. List your name and page number atop each page in case the pages separate.

Avoid Graphics

When designing your cover letter's layout, steer clear of all boxes, shading, and other graphics. If a computer is programmed to avoid graphics and you place information within a graphic, the information will be lost.

Skip Hollow Bullets

If you choose a letter format in which you separate your qualifications line by line, do not use hollow bullets; computers read them as the letter "o." Use solid bullets instead.

No Vertical Lines

Any extra lines in the text can bollix up the type, causing confusion for a scanner. Sometimes the lines are read as the letter "l."

Chapter 14

Ten Tips for Working with Recruiters

In This Chapter

▶ Maximizing benefits from different types of recruiters

▶ Writing computer-friendly cover letters to recruiters

▶ Asking for job descriptions before responding to recruiters

*E*xecutive recruiting is a business with more than its share of fast-talking salespeople — salespeople who can sell you right into the best job of your life.

A specialist in executive recruiting is called an *executive recruiter, executive search consultant, technical recruiter* (if recruiting for technical jobs), and by that colorful term, *headhunter.*

By any name, the recruiter is a third-party professional in the pay of employers. The recruiter is on a mission to find top-of-the-line employees and is not — hear this! — *not* working for you, the job seeker. No matter what a recruiter assures you, the recruiter's loyalty is to the source of business, the employer.

Court Royalty Makers of Corporate America

Executive recruiters can change your life. If they spot your talents and bring you into the spotlight of a client's attention, you can be paired up with some of the best jobs in your career. Make a pile of money, be showered with stock options — all things are possible with executive recruiters.

How do you attract the recruiters who can whisk you to a heaven-sent job?

INSIDER HINT

A backgrounder on third-party employment professionals

Consultants at employment agencies, often called *personnel services*, are third-party professionals who make job matches. Most personnel service searches are paid for by employers; the service finds people for jobs. In a tight job market, a search may be paid for by a job seeker; the service finds jobs for people.

How can you tell the difference between an executive recruiter and an employment agency consultant? With great difficulty. In the old days, recruiters searched outward to fill each position, gathering leads from many sources, while a personnel (employment) service tended to rely more heavily on its own files without doing massive research each time a client was looking for an employee.

The differences have become blurred. Today, many recruiters not only run print recruitment advertising (which only personnel services used to do), but also maintain or subscribe to massive electronic resume databases. So do personnel services.

Another faded difference is that personnel services used to fill jobs paying under $50,000, while the executive recruiters claimed the big-trophy positions. Today, some of the money division remains, but both segments of the industry recruit at six-figures.

The main thing to remember is that (a) unless you are absolutely desperate, don't pay a third-party recruiter or consultant to find you a job, and (b) don't permit your resume to be circulated to employers without your permission.

Start your cultivation of headhunters by running ahead of the crowd. Excel in your position, but go one step further: Arrange to run something that can be measured for results. Publish articles in trade journals and on the Internet. Volunteer for jobs in your professional associations. Be actively involved in maintaining your network of contacts. Send resumes with cover letters to recruiters working in your career area; now that job computers stand guard over resume databases, your self-marketing materials are of vastly more interest than when little mounds of paper had to be sifted manually.

When a recruiter calls you at work, arrange an appointment to call back on your own time. Do not say that you aren't interested. Even if you genuinely do not consider yourself on the market, the job you love may disappear tomorrow. Always talk. If the job isn't for you, offer to suggest other candidates — doing so keeps your lines open for the future.

Generally, recruiters are not interested in anyone earning less than $60,000 a year. More typically, they seek out those earning $100,000 and up, like a $250,000-a-year-job as a marketing VP. Because recruiters are paid high fees to pirate employees in competitive companies, rarely are they interested in spending time with new college graduates. Joblessness is no longer a stigma, so

recruiters will now consider the unemployed as well as employed individuals —
but they'd still rather entice you from a competitor (*somebody else wants you so
you must be good* is the thought).

What about all the community and charity work that once was razzle-dazzle on
a resume? Unfortunately, in this materialistic society, good works don't count
for much when a headhunter calls.

With this backdrop on the topic of executive recruiters, try these ten tips for
working with people who can raise you to the aristocracy of American business.

Understand the Financial Motives of Third-Party Recruiters

Of considerable importance is whether the basic type of recruiting firm you are
dealing with is on contingency or retainer. Both handle high-end people,
although the retainer is better known for finding major corporate chieftains.

A *contingency* recruiting firm is paid only if its candidate is hired. No play, no
pay. Contingency recruiters can be extremely useful in opening employers'
doors. They push hard for their recruits and can circulate your resume to more
than one company at the same time.

By contrast, like a retained legal firm, a *retainer* recruiting firm is paid merely to
search for candidates for a job opening. The firm is paid an agreed-upon fee
regardless of how many candidates they produce or whether their candidates
are hired.

Both contingency and retainer firms offer pros and cons for you.

In the first third of your career, and sometimes later, a contingency firm may
create more action for you. Contingency recruiters can offer you advocacy,
quick action, and wide exposure to many employers. The contingency employer
pushes hard for his or her team — you and perhaps one or two others. You
won't have to wait for Company A to make a decision before being submitted to
Company B. This method is like an auction — the employer who hires first wins
you as a prize.

Retainer firms will not recruit from one client to fill a position at another client
for at least two years. Employees of these client companies are off-limits. If you
work for a client company, no matter how perfect the job at another company,
the retained recruiter will not call your name. To do so would be unethical and
the firm would lose future business.

Save your money

Phony enterprises, masquerading as legitimate executive search firms, scam the unwary. Never pay a "registration fee" or other advance fee to one who claims to be an executive recruiter.

Legitimate recruiters are paid by the client organization for which they are conducting a search. They *never* charge the job seeker.

Further, a retained firm can slow down a job move because the firm only shows you one job opening at a time. Recruiting for Company A must be concluded before you are presented to Company B. If you are unemployed, you risk being presented for a *lesser job opening*. Why? Suppose a retained firm has an important client that every now and then has a marginal job to fill: one that pays a little less or is likely to sunset in a year or two or maybe is located in western Siberia. The recruiter's thinking is, "Why 'waste' a blue-chip employed candidate on a lesser position?"

Nevertheless, when you begin to move up, recruitment dynamics change. Retained recruiters are likely to offer a golden bridge to your future. Because retained recruiters are paid win, lose, or draw, they do not carry a "price tag," as top-flight New York executive recruiter John Lucht explains in his book, *Rites of Passage at $100,000+* (Viceroy/Holt).

If you're moving up but are not quite ready for the retained recruiter level, one way you can protect yourself in an era of changing recruitment prices brought about by technology (company resume databases, for instance) is to personally submit your resume with a cover letter bodyguard to every company where you may like to work. Ask the company to keep your resume on file or in the database for future openings and note that you'll keep it updated periodically.

Give recruiters — both contingency and retained — a list of your favorite companies where your resume is on file. Contingency recruiters will not submit you to these off-limits companies, because they will not earn a fee by doing so — the company already knows about you. Retained recruiters, who have nothing to lose, very well may recommend you, just as they would recommend an outstanding internal candidate.

When dealing with contingency recruiters, insist that your resume is never to be submitted to any employer without your specific permission. The reason for this is that you come with a price tag that can be considerable — say, $25,000 or $30,000. As companies cut costs across the board, another candidate may be found in the backyard of their database — or on the Internet — for a lot less money. You then are priced out of the running, and you'll probably never know why.

Even when you're a RedHot candidate, you can benefit by working with contingency recruiters. The ideal situation is when the recruiter has a directive to fill a position you wouldn't have contacted on your own — one that you may never even have heard about.

Finally, check out the recruiting company's credentials. If the firm is sizable, see if it's a member of the *Association of Executive Search Consultants* (AESC). Lots of good recruiters choose not to belong, but members are required to adhere to guidelines protecting the interests of both the client and the recruit. For a comprehensive list of executive recruiters, refer to the *Directory of Executive Recruiters* (Consultants News, Fitzwilliam, N.H.), which indexes by career area as well as alphabetically.

Match Your Background to the Recruiter's Specialty

Recruiters specialize. Find out which firms recruit in your career area. Just as you would for any other cover letter, try to showcase your qualifications that best meet the recruiter's needs.

Ask Recruiters for Position's Job Description

Ring, ring! A recruiter is on the telephone saying that you sound like a candidate for a terrific opportunity. If you currently have a good job that you're reasonably happy with, play it safe. Make sure that a better job is available before you send out your resume.

When a recruiter hands your resume and cover letter to a client, the general assumption may be that you can be had. Consequently, if your resume is sent to too many businesses, this assumption could become widespread. Overexposing your resume in this manner can have serious consequences, especially if your resume gets back to your employer, who may not be particularly amused by your itchiness.

Some unscrupulous recruiting firms have been known to go *fishing* — seeking resumes with no specific available positions in mind — as a method of drumming up business. They use your resume to impress potential clients into signing their company as recruiting consultants. Such firms often send out your resume to potential clients across the country without your knowledge or approval. In some cases, they even fudge your qualifications and change your job requirements behind your back.

Make sure that a recruiting firm asking you for personal information (as in willingness to move, salary, and so on) has a specific job in mind. Find out such details as information about the hiring company, the responsibilities of the position, its place in the company organization, and the relationship between the recruiter and the company. Ask for the position's job description. (In addition to verifying a valid search, you need the description to devise a compatible cover letter and resume.)

If possible, get these details in writing. If the recruiter is unwilling to give this information, you may want to end the conversation right then and there.

Answer All Questions Honestly

You and the recruiter share this one objective: to avoid a bad fit. Both of you have much to lose by mispackaging your qualifications. If the recruiter regularly scouts employees for a given company, the recruiter is likely to know if the new position is one that could blow up in your face. You're going to lay out your goals, ambitions, heart's desires, and other private matters; in return, grill the recruiter to find out what you want to know.

Write Computer-Friendly Cover Letters and Resumes

Recruiting firms may inventory thousands of resumes. Computers that scan resumes and cover letters are becoming as common as fax machines. Make reading your qualifications easy for a computer. See Chapter 13 for tips on making your letters computer-friendly.

Be Cogent and Concise

Like corporate hiring managers, recruiters are not interested in details on a par with hearing how you were mentally scarred when your brother ambushed you with water balloons at the tender age of five. Pretend each extraneous fact costs you $100; each extraneous word costs you $25.

Willing to Relocate? Say So

This tip may seem pretty basic, but emphasizing your geographical flexibility helps — if you mean it. If you decide you really don't want to live in Upper Icebox, find another reason to turn down the job a recruiter has just spent three weeks trying to make happen with you.

Reveal Your Salary History

Unlike your general strategy to duck salary history and requirements until you've been offered a job, be candid with bona fide executive recruiters — and if you are asked to send in tax statement proof of your earnings, say clearly that you expect the earnings history to be kept confidential between the recruiter and the employer.

Like Middle East peace, salary is always a difficult subject to negotiate. Suppose the recruiter asks that you send a marketing package, including your salary history or requirements.

With history, state the cash compensation as a separate item, adding your benefit package as a second figure — perhaps 30 to 40 percent of your salary. Recruiters are too sophisticated to buy the "total compensation" statement in which you combine your salary, benefits, anticipated salary, and anything else you can think of to swell the figure.

As for salary requirements, if you avoid giving any figure at all when requested in your cover letter, you probably won't be considered by the recruiter. (This probability is not true when you are dealing directly with employers.) Giving a single figure can make you look inflexible. By stating a range of salary expectations, you can give the recruiter a good gauge of your market value, while allowing room to negotiate. See Chapter 16 for more about the salary issue.

Keep a Record of All Contacts with Recruiters

Keep copies of all written correspondence and telephone conversations with recruiters. You never know when you'll need to have a record of the negotiations that took place.

Don't Depend on Recruiters for Your Job Search

This fact can't be emphasized enough: *a recruiter's responsibility is to the employer, not to you.* A recruiter is not in business to find you a job, but, rather, to find new employees for client companies.

Having said that, recruiters are a good way to jump start your job search. Start with a direct mail campaign to relevant executive search firm consultants. The mail campaign can be working for you while you get organized to network and read recruitment ads. The mailing campaign may produce as many as 10 to 30 responses on a 300- to 500-piece mailing — a real morale booster.

Once you submit your resume to a recruiter, do not make independent contacts with the client without the recruiter's knowledge. Not only will this tactic probably backfire on the particular job, but it may also cause you to be black-listed by the recruiting firm in the long run.

Chapter 15

Ten Hints for Answering Job Ads

In This Chapter

▶ Sleuthing the Internet and other resources

▶ Reflecting the ad in your cover letter

▶ Opening the box on blind ads

---

*T*oday's recruitment ads are a gold mine of information about jobs *immediately available.*

Printed media — newspapers and trade journals — are far and away the chief place to find recruitment advertising, but Internet recruitment ads are making significant inroads.

Some researchers estimate that no less than 10 percent of all available job openings appear in print, either in newspapers or professional trade journals, or online in the electronic universe. But even if the figure is so low (and that's debatable), millions of jobs are filled by recruitment advertising each year.

As for the Internet, one site alone, *America's Job Bank*, the Labor Department's World Wide Web site, is working its way toward piping one million job openings a day through its facility — jobs that anyone with a computer and modem can access. Add to that number the hundreds of thousands of jobs listed by a wide diversity of Internet Web resources, ranging from the National Association of Colleges and Employers' *JobWeb* to the nonprofit consortium of employers operating the *Online Career Center,* and you can see that recruitment advertising is thunderously important in your job search.

Do cover letters relate in the same way to printed advertisements and online job postings? Most of the time, yes.

Always enclose a cover letter when you answer a printed job advertisement. Usually enclose a cover letter when you answer an online job posting, but read the instructions on the posting. Sometimes the job posting says "resumes only" or "no cover letter required." Or you'll merely be asked to fill in an online job application form. Unless the instructions ask you to omit a cover letter, send the best one you can write. On the Internet, the world is your competition.

Even if you do not find a job in the help-wanted ads so picture perfect you could frame it, scanning these ads can help you determine the characteristics of the current job market so that you get fresh ammunition for the cover letters you do write.

Repeated advertising for applicants with certain technical experience indicates the current level of training that's in demand. Many companies that advertise are expanding — if they ask for environmental engineers, they may also want mechanical engineers and administrative assistants. You can also determine which professions are searching for applicants from advertisements. For example, if you're a secretary and you find ten openings for legal secretaries and only two for medical secretaries, you may want to learn more about legal terminology before you write your cover letters.

Take these hints to heart as you respond to recruitment advertising.

Let Your Letter Reflect the Ad's KeyWords or Skill Phrases

For an office position, an employer may require knowledge of *word processing*, and even specific programs like Microsoft Word or WordPerfect. Engineers may need experience with certain *computer-aided drafting and design software*. Travel agents may need familiarity with ticket reservation systems. When an advertisement mentions specific qualifications — and you have them — showcase the qualifications in your letter. If the ad mentions general KeyWords such as *professional* or *creative*, describe yourself and your record with these exact terms.

Mine the Ad for Information about the Employer

Perhaps you hadn't thought of job ads in this way, but an advertisement acts as the employer's cover letter. Advertisements accentuate the positive, attracting attention with strong points while ignoring potential weaknesses.

Checking the ad itself is revealing. The following tips do not apply to Internet ads, but are important for printed ads.

✔ Is the ad large? This company may be flush with money and pay its people well — or it may be such a poor place to work that high turnover requires constant recruiting.

✔ Is the ad small? Maybe the firm is new and has a low advertising budget, in which case you could get a jump on the competition by getting in early. Or, if the company is small but undergoing expansion, maybe you should respond to the contact named in the ad, but at the same time, directly contact the hiring manager for whom you would work.

✔ A blind ad could indicate that a huge response is expected or that a senior-level position is about to open up.

Now that the Internet has made communication within a community much easier, join a Net discussion group and ask if any members have heard of the company and what they can tell you about it. Soon you'll have strong clues about which is the most powerful information to put in your cover letter. If the Internet is new to you, take a look at *The Internet For Dummies* from IDG Books Worldwide, Inc.

Refer to the Advertisement Early

Telling the employer how you learned of an opening is always good. Doing so immediately establishes that you are applying for a position the company intends to fill in the near future. A convenient place to put this information is to the right of the inside address in a "RE[garding]" statement.

Customize Your Letter for Each Employer

You are responding to a particular ad for a particular job opening, so tailor your letter to the requirements the employer lists. A customized letter has a much higher chance of a positive response.

Use a Linear Format When You're a Good Match

If you possess a substantial number of the qualifications the ad requests, show those qualifications line by line. This concept is illustrated in a number of Chapter 11's model cover letters.

Use a Paragraph Format When You're a Marginal Match

Organize your letter in the literary, or paragraph, format if you lack a few qualifications or experience pertinent to the job. Paragraphing allows you to emphasize your strengths at the beginning of paragraphs, sending readers on an archaeological dig to find your weaknesses buried deep inside the text — if they can find them at all. An advertisement lists qualifications for the ideal candidate, but the ideal candidate is not always available.

Address Your Letter to a Specific Individual

Dear Somebody beats *Dear Nobody*. When the advertisement lists no name, call and scout it out. You may need to be resourceful, as companies are often closemouthed. Be persistent. Chapter 2 has some tips for tracking down hard-to-find names.

Be Resourceful in Replying to Blind Ads

Play detective to find out the employer's name when you respond to a blind ad with no clue as to the employer's identity. For newspaper ads, you may be able to find out the name of the box holder at a U.S. post office (see Chapter 2). If the box is at a commercial company, make friends with the counter clerk; you may be able to pry the information loose. If the box is at a publication, such as a newspaper, you're probably out of luck. (Although I do know a young man who waited in a lobby where box mail was picked up, listened to hear the box number called, and then followed the messenger back to the company. Generally, this method is a big waste of time.)

Trade journal ads tend to be national, making it difficult to track down the identity of the advertising company in another city.

You can't find out the advertiser's identity in a blind ad posted on the Internet that comes through a commercial service such as *E-Span*. The commercial service uses confidential logs to protect the advertiser's preference for anonymity. When a blind ad is posted on a public site, such as the newsgroup `misc.jobs.misc`, you may be able to use the Internet location-finding tools, *Whois* and *Finger,* to uncover the company's name.

Focus on Experience Directly Related to the Job

Just as you would in any RedHot cover letter, shine a spotlight on just the benefits you have that the employer wants. No extras.

Mail Your Letters on Sunday or Monday

Some advisers suggest that your letter gets more attention if you wait until the initial flood of replies has subsided before responding to an advertisement. They may be right. But in an ever-thinner job market, my advice is to move on a job you want right away. Get a jump on the competition. Get something out the same day you see the ad, or, at the latest, the next day.

What the words really mean

No self-respecting cover letter book can go to press without a few prankful peeks at what advertising words really mean to some people in the deep underbelly of the job market.

entry-level job.

You'll have to work two jobs to get in out of the cold.

up-and-coming company.

It's a start-up operation, and already the company is on the edge of bankruptcy.

requires leadership skills.

We need you to be our enforcer.

requires some overtime.

Some overtime every night and every weekend.

requires problem-solving skills.

Management creates a problem and requires you to solve it.

I know how to deal with pressure situations.

I hide under my desk chugging pots of coffee.

I have a great sense of humor.

I spend the entire day telling old jokes.

I have strong communication skills.

I talk too much.

I take pride in the work I do.

When I do something wrong, I blame someone else.

I mesh well with co-workers.

I'm a gossip.

I'm motivated to succeed.

I don't want to work for this joke of a company any longer than I absolutely have to.

Chapter 16

Ten Tips for Handling the Salary Issue

. . . .

In This Chapter

▶ Understanding new total compensation packages
▶ Dealing with premature requests for salary data
▶ Using new online sources to find what jobs pay

. . . .

*T*o guess is cheap. To guess wrong is expensive.

— old Chinese proverb

Money talk isn't the same as in times past. Until the 1990s, when changes in pay systems spread rapidly, most white-collar job seekers found new jobs and negotiated only a specified salary — *base pay*. Upper-level executives were the only ones to receive deal-sweetening bonuses and stock options.

Today, the name of the game is *total compensation* — base pay, variable pay, and indirect pay.

Variable pay is the bonus concept. Previously reserved for management, this type of pay is now available for all levels of employees. In the past five years, what employers have been willing to spend on base pay has dropped 27 percent, while bonuses have risen 79 percent.

Indirect pay, formerly referred to as employee fringe benefits, often constitutes as much as one-third of an individual's base pay.

To ensure that you're paid at market rate for your new job (after the offer), find out the details about bonuses and employee benefits, combined with base pay, that are offered as part of your total compensation package. As an applicant for a position, you sell a part of your life to an employer; aim for a fair return.

Employers hire people with specific skills, knowledge, and work methods to make a profit, leading the way for *skill-based pay* and *knowledge-based pay*.

To get what you deserve means you need to understand — even speak — the New Pay jargon. *Broadbanding* and *performance-based pay* illustrate compensation buzzwords making the rounds throughout office halls everywhere. (See the "Understanding contemporary compensation jargon: A glossary" sidebar.)

Here are some tips for dealing with premature salary requests. Pay close attention — this advice could bring you extra thousands of dollars. You deserve to make what you're *qualified* to make.

TECHNICAL STUFF

Understanding contemporary compensation jargon: A glossary

Base pay: Pay before any addition of differentials, allowances, or incentives for foreign service or required contributions.

Broadbanding: As organizations flatten and people move sideways instead of up, they become unhappy if their salaries drop with a new assignment. In the traditional pay structure (perhaps 25 grades), a salary cut can happen. A broadbanded pay structure (perhaps 3 to 5 grades), solves the pay problems of lateral transfer because all employees in a band are paid similarly.

A more formal definition is given by Hewitt Associates' Kenan S. Abosch, broadbanding guru and author of *Improving Organizational Effectiveness Through Broadbanding* (American Compensation Association):

> *Broadbanding is a term used when many traditional salary grades are collapsed into a few wide "bands" for purposes of managing career growth and administering pay. By eliminating much of the hierarchy associated with a traditional pay structure, it supports today's flatter, leaner, more customer-focused organization.*

Gainsharing: Any one of a number of incentive programs designed to share productivity gains with employees as a group.

Gross-up: The practice of increasing the amount of a cash payment to offset the tax impact to the individual resulting from the cash payment.

Indirect pay: All forms of nondirect (noncash) compensation provided to employees in exchange for their contribution to an organization.

Job-based pay: Pay based on job responsibilities, not skills.

Knowledge-based pay: A system of salary differentiation based on the formal education, related experience, or specialized training a professional employee has that qualifies the individual to deal with specific subject matter, or work effectively in a specific field. Salary level may not be dependent on whether the incumbent uses the knowledge.

Performance-based pay: A compensation program designed to pay employees according to on-the-job performance.

Skill-based pay: A person-based compensation system based on the variety of jobs an employee performs rather than the specific job the employee may be doing at a particular time. Pay increases are associated with the addition and/or improvement of an individual's skills, as opposed to better performance or seniority within the system. Pay level generally is not dependent on whether any of the skills are utilized.

Variable pay: Any rewards given to employees for performance that contributes to the success of the organization.

SOURCE: BASED ON THE AMERICAN COMPENSATION ASSOCIATION'S *GLOSSARY OF COMPENSATION AND BENEFITS TERMS*, 1995, EXCEPT THE TERM "BROADBANDING," used with permission.

Don't Give Away Salary Issues in Your Cover Letter

Whether you are responding to a recruitment advertisement asking for salary history or to cite your salary expectations, save this information for the interview. Admittedly, some interviewers will not consider your application unless you believe the ad and reveal private and personal financial information in your letter. Most advocates for job seekers agree that if your responding letter and resume are outstanding, leaving off the salary information is unlikely to screen you out of good places to work.

My rule for responding to a premature request for salary history and requirement is

Stall salary talk until you get the job offer.

Until you have an offer, the employer holds all the cards. Once you have an offer, you know you have something the employer wants and the dynamics change. You become equals negotiating a business proposition.

Listing salary information in your cover letter weakens your bargaining position. A salary too low devalues your abilities; a salary too high looks like you're too big for the company. Both scenarios leave you out of luck.

Tell Recruiters Your Salary Information

The only time you should answer a salary question before you're offered a job is when asked by third-party employment specialists — executive or technical recruiters and employment consultants, for instance. These professionals are paid for their time, just like lawyers and physicians. They are too busy to waste precious hours with you if you don't make recommending you to clients easy for them. Too many other people are standing in line for the job you want, ready to tell all if you play coy.

Don't Inflate Your Salary History

Suppose that you're asked to reveal your salary history in your cover letter. Three schools of thought exist on this issue: those who recommend reporting base pay and variable pay, others who suggest that you lump salary and benefits together for one figure, and yet another camp of advisors — with whom I agree — who say:

> *Show compensation in modules. List base pay and variable pay in one figure; give another figure for indirect pay; and then add the figures together for the total compensation package.*

What to Do If You Have to Spill the Beans Early

Even if you have to tell, you don't have to be specific.

> *State your figures in wide ranges so that you're not excluded from consideration for positions for which you are qualified.*

Include figures slightly above and below the market value for the position to cover all your bases.

Analyze Requests for Proof of Salary

You thought the fact that your prospective employer asked what you're currently making was enough, but what do you do about requests for *proof* — asking that you enclose a copy of your W-2 form in your application?

An employer can legally ask for your W-2 form. That's the only thing career insiders agree on. One school of thought is that the employer — especially those who hire sales personnel working on commission — is entitled to see your proof of earnings. Others, including myself, see such requests as an invasion of privacy and a presumption that you are a liar.

At the cover letter stage, I can't imagine you would want to release your earnings information, especially in response to a blind box ad. Negotiation whiz Jack Chapman put it well in his book, *How to Make $1000 a Minute* (in bookstores or from the author at 847-251-4727). Write something like the following in your cover letter:

> *I understand you've requested a salary history; I'm paid roughly the market-value of a (job title) with (#) years' experience, and while I'm not willing to publish my compensation package, I'd be happy to discuss it with you during an interview.*

(If the employer calls to say no interview until you "follow instructions" and cough up your salary history, ask for a mutual exchange: *I'll show you mine if you show me yours!* — just kidding.) The exception to this rule is that giving your tax document or final pay stub of the year to a recruiter is okay, for reasons noted above.

My conclusion: Focus your efforts on employers who trust you more, meaning those who don't request your W-2.

Write Lines that Skirt the Salary Issue

Here are some suggestions to dodge the salary issue until you're in the interview.

Remember, these statements and others like them won't advance you to the candidate pool unless your cover letter and resume are superb. Your self-marketing package must establish you as a RedHot candidate.

- ✔ *What I've learned so far about the position suggests that it really fits me, so if you pay a fair market value, I don't foresee any problems with salary. Why don't we arrange an interview, and we can discuss salary then?*

- ✔ *Assuming your position is appropriately compensated, we'll surely be able to agree on a figure.*

- ✔ *I'll be happy to discuss my salary information when we meet to review my skills and your needs.*

- ✔ *Once we discuss some of the successes I've achieved in handling this sort of position, there should be no problem. All I require is a fair market value for the position, and I'm sure that you pay that, so let's meet to discuss the position; salary will take care of itself later.*

> ✔ When we've had a chance to discuss what I can contribute to your position, then I'm sure that we'll be able to work out appropriate compensation that we both feel good about.
>
> ✔ After we've taken a look at how closely my skills and experience fit your needs, I'll be glad to provide complete salary information.
>
> ✔ You should know that my total compensation has ranged between ($) and ($) in recent years.
>
> ✔ If your compensation is based on performance, we'll find agreement easy when you see the benefits I bring to the job.

Find Out Your Market Value

Knowing your market value is the centerpiece for negotiating the compensation you deserve. Market value is the going rate for people in your industry with skills similar to yours who are doing virtually the same job as you.

People tend to treat their earnings like a national security issue. But you can find pay rates by looking up salary studies in printed publications. And now — for the first time! — you can also find a lot of salary data online. Both types of resources are discussed later in this chapter. You may have to use several studies, plus do a little guessing to pinpoint good figures in your locale. Your research efforts are well worth your time.

If you don't know the right price, how are you going to ask for it?

Where to Find Pay Information in Print

Try a library for career books with pay figures; watch for magazines such as *U.S. News & World Report, Working Woman,* and *Parade,* which annually publish reports on salaries.

Read recruitment advertisements, looking for earnings data. Read civil service postings at public job service offices and libraries — pay may be similar to comparable jobs in private industry.

Public employment service offices may have regional or state compensation studies for jobs in the private sector.

Or check with your state's occupational information coordinating committee (OICC) for occupational outlook statements that often include salary information; call 202-653-5665 for the contact person and telephone number for your state's OICC. Many states publish occupational outlook statements and will send a free copy upon request.

Read the trade press. For instance, *Chemical Engineering & News* publishes salary surveys for chemical engineers. *The Scientist* does stories about median annual salaries of scientists.

Most professional societies and trade associations conduct salary studies among members. The information may or may not be available to nonmembers. If you don't belong to the appropriate organization, consider joining. Look them up in *The Encyclopedia of Associations* in your library.

A private firm, Abbott, Langer & Associates, conducts surveys on employee compensation, benefits, and working conditions. They supply comprehensive reports for a fee: Abbott, Langer & Associates, 548 First Street, Crete, IL 60417; telephone: 708-672-4200. An overview of salary studies is available free online (see the section "Where to Find Salary Information Online").

A number of private compensation firms and research organizations, such as Towers Perrin and the American Management Association, publish massive salary studies. These generally are not available to the public or to libraries. If you have a friend in a human resources department or recruiting firm, you may be able to find the information you need.

Where to Find Salary Information Online

A new world is opening in salary data that you can obtain on the Internet to discover the market rate for the kind of work you do. What follows is a sampling of the early starters — expect many more online salary resources within the next year. Professional societies, as a single example, are beginning to establish World Wide Web pages for their fields, which generally include salary talk.

Electronic postings at most Web sites are free; in some cases you can access additional information for a fee. Try these Internet World Wide Web sites:

JobSmart, a stunning nonprofit resource, launched with federal grant money to California Bay Area public libraries, that puts more than 70 salary surveys a mouse click away. JobSmart links to other sites provide other information as well, ranging from salary negotiation fundamentals to a relocation salary calculator that helps you learn the changes in costs of living from one U.S. locale to another. See it at:

```
http://jobsmart.org
```

JobWeb, operated by the National Association of Colleges and Employers, publishes an overview of salaries for new college graduates by career field. You'll find it at:

```
http://www.jobweb.org
```

Institute of Management and Administration's (IOMA) Report on Salary Surveys, a periodical for compensation specialists and human resource managers. Recent reports covered secretaries, logistics managers, and accounting staff. A new occupation is posted each month. See IOMA at:

```
http://www.enews.com/magazines/rss/
```

The Bureau of Labor Statistics, a government agency within the U.S. Department of Labor, posts full surveys, economic and regional information, research and feedback for a variety of career fields. Access this information at:

```
http://stats.bls.gov/
```

Source Services Corporation, a commercial company, supplies surveys for computer, engineering, accounting and finance fields. Full surveys, case studies, career trends, compensation data, job responsibilities, and networking information are available at:

```
http://www.espan.com/salary/
```

National Engineering Search (NES), a recruiting firm, offers yet more salary information on engineers: aerospace/defense, automotive, chemical, computers, and industrial equipment. Look at a partial overview of the salary survey:

```
http://www.nesnet.com/salary.html
```

Creative Financial (CF) Staffing, a recruiting firm, posts accountant salary surveys. Positions cited include accounting manager, senior accountant, staff accountant, and accounting clerk. Access this information at:

```
http://www.cfstaffing.com/salary.html
```

The Society for Human Resource Management, a membership society for specialists in human resources: employee assistant manager, work and family program manager, and wellness program manager, for instance. Partial results are posted at:

```
http://www.shrm.org/docs/magazine/chart4.html
```

Abbott, Langer & Associates, a private compensation research firm, posts salary overviews for sales and marketing managers, engineering, information systems managers, lawyers, financial executives, human resource executives, banking managers, laboratory assistants, drafting supervisors and more.

See the numbers at:

```
http://205.164.8.12/~glanger/ala/ala.html
```

Chapter 17

Ten Ways to Handle Your References' Buzz

In This Chapter
▶ Finding out what references say about you
▶ Reference checking: what's legal, what's not
▶ Dealing with poor references

*W*hen new movies come out, the question is: *What's the buzz about it?*—*buzz* meaning how people are rating the film.

Have you ever wondered what's the employment buzz about you — what past employers say when asked for a reference? No matter how RedHot your cover letters, a poor reference can be a knock-out punch in your job search. Fortunately, letters can also help when you suspect that a past employer is sabotaging your chances for a new work connection. You do have options, some of which depend upon writing letters.

The following ten tips take you on a behind-the-scenes tour of the business of reference auditing. They've been reviewed by employment attorney Sheldon Weinhaus of St. Louis, Missouri.

Understand What's Legal, What's Not

On the advice of their lawyers, many employers when asked for references about former employees respond with as few words as possible. They stick to the minimal documented facts — for example, position title, dates of employment, final salary, attendance record, and production record.

If employers do veer beyond the bare bones and reveal negative information about former employees, they need to provide specific details supporting the damaging data, and they cannot release the information with malicious intent. For example, employers cannot recommend that you not be hired, but they can state that they received four letters from co-workers requesting that they not be placed on work teams with you.

Moreover, employers cannot provide unsolicited information. Legally, they can only answer specific questions. So, if a reference checker asks why you were fired, former employers can answer that question. But they cannot provide such information unless asked, or they open themselves up to a defamation lawsuit. In addition, the reason for the firing must not only be true but provable (potentially to a jury) — personal opinion isn't enough.

Although the minimal-information policy cuts down on the chance that employers will give you a negative reference, it also discourages employers from giving you a good reference. Many companies have adopted an ironclad policy of clamming up, no matter what kind of employee you had been.

What a reference checker cannot do legally is obtain information about arrest records — although arrest record databases have been openly advertised and sold to employers in the past.

Don't Count on Employer Silence

Although various studies suggest that employers do not do nearly the amount of checking you might expect, fudging on your credentials and background can boomerang.

So how many companies bother to check references in depth? I don't think anyone knows the answer for certain, but stories in the human resources trade press claim that reference checking is on the rise.

Another side of the coin is that, although previous employers may be reluctant to give negative references for fear of being sued, they are also vulnerable to *negligent hiring* lawsuits in which a foreseeable injury occurs because a former employer kept quiet about a negative fact. To illustrate, a company was sued for failure to tell the hiring employer that the employee in question was fired for theft. The employee stole again. The hiring company argued that the reference had an obligation to be honest and forthcoming about the crime.

In today's marketplace, the employer can be sued either way — for defaming a former employee or for covering up a significant negative fact. Never assume a previous employer will remain silent about your past sins.

Know the Companies That Do Check References

If you have a splotched past that will negatively affect your chances for another job, you can try to avoid the issue entirely and apply at companies where they probably will not check your references. Stick to small companies, list your true work history, and hope to slide by.

Avoid the following employers, who are likely to scrutinize your references carefully: companies with well-staffed human resource departments, financial institutions, high-tech companies, and government contractors. Also expect to have references checked if you have not held a similar job to the one you applied for, or if you have an atypical job-changing pattern.

Understand How Credit Reports Can Hurt You

Most employees are not subject to credit reports but painful things happen as a result of negative credit reports, including those based on mistaken identity.

When a job is not financially sensitive, why do companies pay for credit checks? They say it's because a credit report contains much more than just payment history. It offers data, from names of past employers to residential stability. It describes divorces and estimated prior earnings. If the reference checker makes certain assumptions about values, a credit check is said to show a pattern of your lifestyle.

What about a bankruptcy? The Bankruptcy Code's Section 525(b) prohibits private employers from refusing to hire or from discriminating against an individual because of bankruptcy. (Obtain a copy of the code from a library or from your member of Congress.) Having said that, discrimination on the basis of bankruptcy occurs, but employers won't admit that's the reason. Proving it is tough.

What your credit report shows is correlated to what you have said. Disparities brand you as unreliable. Suppose you have moved around a lot — employers will wonder why.

When you are denied employment (within the last 60 days) and you suspect the denial is credit related, you may be entitled to a free credit report. Otherwise, you'll pay a modest fee to see your credit files. Check with your local credit bureau first, but details of obtaining your credit report are available from the Big Three credit systems by toll-free telephoning: Equifax, 800-685-1111; Transunion, 800-851-2674; TRW, 800-682-7654.

Job applications routinely contain a clause giving the employer the right to run a credit check. Denying permission raises a red flag.

Know What Background Checks May Include

Employers hire investigators to compile dossiers on very few candidates because the exhaustive checkups are expensive. They're only ordered for big jobs or security-clearance government work. Investigators, however, may be retained to search out certain public record details, such as employment and school records, motor-vehicle histories, insurance claims, and courthouse records.

Public record searches may also be ordered to spot large medical claims or a sizable worker's compensation award. Increasingly, public record reporting is done by computer searches.

Beware of Incorrect Professional Reference Checks

Some employers hire companies that search a range of databases to assemble informational profiles of applicants. Mistakes are sometimes made.

The big companies in the business try to be very careful, but even they can go out to lunch. The employee screening service may make a minor error in the spelling of your name and uncover information about someone else that it then applies to you.

A few years ago, a newsmagazine reported the story of a man who was fired for a cocaine conviction six weeks after starting a new job. As it turned out, a major firm that investigated had inadvertently pulled the criminal record of another man with a similar name by mistake.

If your name is a very common one, you might add this postscript to your thank-you-for-the-interview letter:

> *P.S. As you know, database errors are made from time to time, such as a confusion of names. (I sometimes receive mail meant for another with my name.) Because my record and references are excellent, I hope you'll let me know if any information turns up casting a shadow on my candidacy for this job, for which I have ideal qualifications. That would give me a chance to correct any inaccuracies. Thanks.*

Ask a Friend to Sleuth

Employers large enough to have lawyers and a human resource department usually keep their lips zipped about negative information. Staff at smaller companies may not realize the legal slippery slope upon which they find themselves when they badmouth a former employee.

If you suspect that a former supervisor is grinding you into dust, ask a friend to call and find out what's being said. Choose a business friend — preferably one who knows the lingo of your field or of employment services — to contact your past employers and conduct a pretend reference check. Prime your friend to ask specific questions about you and your past performance with the company and to keep notes with the answers.

If you are receiving negative references from a former supervisor, the easiest way to handle the issue is to neutralize the references. Even if you hate the supervisor's guts, visit your old bosses, say that you may fail to get a job because of the references, belly crawl, and appeal to a sense of fair play. If it was your fault, ask for compassion. (With luck, you won't have to see that person again in your entire lifetime.)

If you succeed in getting your former boss to interpret your previous employment in a more favorable light, do write a letter of thanks immediately. The letter serves as a reminder of the truce.

Learn Strategies to Combat Negative References

When neutralizing your ex-bosses doesn't work and you know you're going to get negative references, perhaps justifiably, take measures to decrease their significance.

✔ When you leave a job, get a letter of reference from someone who knows your work history and performance. Draft it yourself if you can.

✔ Use your writing skills to compile a list of testimonials in addition to your reference sheet. Edit these testimonials down to punchy statements of several lines in length. Find testimonial nuggets in performance reviews and from documents and letters you've saved from a variety of people. Put names to the testimonials and verify permission to use them with the people who spoke the words. Make your career look like an open book by giving references' complete and current addresses (residential, business, and e-mail) and telephone numbers. This gives the impression that you have nothing to hide.

✔ Write to a list of references. Fellow members of trade associations, members of related departments of previous positions you've held, colleagues, friends in high places, or connections in the prospective employer's company or circle of friends. Coach these people to comment favorably on your ability to pitch in and help on projects, get along with people, and generally be likable. This is especially important if you've had a firefight with a previous boss.

Know When to Call a Lawyer

Even if you don't want to get involved in a lawsuit, you may benefit from contacting a lawyer. When you know that a previous employer is giving unsolicited, malicious, or irrelevant information, ask a lawyer to write a letter on the law firm's letterhead requesting your ex-employer to stop the libel (injury to your reputation) — or else. This action will cost you anywhere from $50 to $200 but it's more affordable than a full-blown defamation suit and, based on my observation, it usually works.

Don't Panic — One Bad Reference Probably Won't Hurt Your Chances

If an employer checks several of your references and only one of them is negative, chances are you're still in the running for the job.

It's not the one-time clash that matters; it's the buzz — the pattern of what several references have to say about your behavior.

What if the buzz about you is bad everywhere? You may find it easier to start in a temporary position and hope that by good example you'll eventually be offered a job on the regular payroll.

Chapter 18

Ten Burned-Out Words and Phrases

● ●

In This Chapter

▶ Avoiding all-too-familiar phrases

▶ Using words that turn your letter into a hot property

● ●

*O*ut of the frying pan and into the fire. When it rains, it pours. The acid test. Eyeball it (as a verb). Feedback. Hands-on. Meaningful. Point in time. Richly deserved. State of the art. Once these phrases had significance, but they've been penalized for their popularity. Now these tired words need a nap. Potential employers will probably yawn if you succumb to Burned-Out phrases like these:

✔ **I am very interested in —**

This phrase is usually followed by a mention of your occupation or career field — either the one you're in or the one you want to be in. If you weren't interested, you wouldn't be writing in the first place. Let this phrase rest in peace.

✔ **I am forwarding the enclosed resume for your consideration —**

Why else would you send a resume? To light a fire to keep out the winter cold?

✔ **I feel that I have —**

Feelings. Nice song — no business meaning. Nothing more than feelings.

✔ **I am energetic.**

Who would say "I am lethargic"? If you make this kind of statement, don't let the statement stand alone — back it up with details.

✔ **Please find the enclosed resume...**

Is the resume lost? Finding your enclosed resume is not quite like searching for the Lost City of the Incas. Your resume is right there in the same envelope you sent the cover letter in. Or is it? You did remember to *enclose* the resume, didn't you?

✔ **Salary requirements are negotiable.**

Avoid using this phrase as a stand alone statement. When you're asked to reveal your salary requirements, try to avoid doing so, but add the richness of detail described in Chapter 16.

✔ **I am responding to your advertisement.**

Nothing is really wrong with this line, except that it has tire tracks all over it. This phrase comes complete with all the excitement of watching grass grow. Use the line if you must, but put as much effort as you can into coming up with something fresher.

✔ **I look forward to hearing from you.**

Why do you assume the hiring authority will contact you? You may end up looking forward for a long time. Hang onto control — you make the follow-up contact.

✔ **Please accept the enclosed resume.**

What does this phrase mean — please accept the resume and make a paper airplane out of it, file it away, read it, burn it, what? Do you expect your resume to be marked "Return to sender"?

✔ **Utilize my expertise in —**

Don't just claim to have proficiency in a particular subject. *Prove* your expertise. Show your accomplishments. Explain what you did.

Ten overweight clichés

First priority

Priority says the same thing.

Go ahead and take action

Take action spells out your meaning.

Honest truth

Truth is enough.

Mixed together

Mixed will do.

Open up

Open is plenty.

Past history

History suffices.

Point in time

Time covers the thought.

Reason why

Reason explains fully.

Refer back to

Refer to handles the question.

This particular job

This job is all you need.

Appendix
Problem Words

*W*hat's the difference between *its* and *it's*? When do you use *among* instead of *between*? Can you remember how many *c*'s and *m*'s are in the word *recommend* without dashing to the nearest dictionary?

If you can't answer these questions, join the crowd! (If you can, give yourself a prize and enjoy your relative freedom from dictionary dementia.) The English language creates problems for everyone. Whether dealing with spelling, commonly confused words, or strict definitions that get loosened in everyday conversation, everybody needs a little help now and then.

Don't let your cover letter fall prey to embarrassing mistakes in word usage or spelling. At worst, creative spelling or unique usage will spiral your missive into the Bermuda Triangle of cover letters. At best, you'll provide the recipient with a gaggle of giggles at your expense.

I can't promise to turn you into a word-wielding impresario, but using this guide will clear up confusing and misused language so that you can craft a credible cover letter. Look up the words you've chosen for your cover letter (don't skip the *a*'s and *an*'s — you may be surprised) and master their meanings. And if you don't remember later, no problem! Just look them up again.

a/an: The use of these two words has nothing to do with how a word is spelled but rather with how it sounds. Use *a* with words that begin with a consonant sound and *an* with words that begin with a vowel sound.

ability: See *capacity/ability*.

-able/-ible: These suffixes are a doozy when it comes to spelling. Look the words up in a dictionary because no hard and fast rules exist for determining the correct spelling. Be alert to words that are spelled alike except for the suffix ending.

able: Use this word only with active verbs. If you've used it with a passive, or being, verb, replace it with *can*. Ex: Write "I *can* do it" not "I am *able* to do it."

about: *About* is commonly used in place of *almost*. Be more accurate.

about/approximately: *Approximately* is a better word choice because it's more formal and implies greater accuracy. Using *about* may sound like you're guessing or hedging.

above: A term that tends toward the pretentious. Phrases like "Pay attention to *the above*" sound really stuffy. Use *this* or *that* with a reference. See also *aforementioned*.

absolutely: People often use this adverb to intensify their pronouncements. If you want to impress someone, use tangible experiences rather than flimsy adverbs.

absolutes: Absolutes are words that allow for no degree or comparison, such as *perfect*, *unanimous*, *always*, and *absolute*. Use these words only if you know that you can back them up with documented information. Otherwise, qualify them with *almost* or *nearly*.

accent marks: When spelling foreign words that have been adopted into English, omitting the accent marks is OK, although many people still use them to aid pronunciation.

accompanied: When used in reference to people, use the preposition *by*. If referring to things, use *with*.

accompanied by: When you use this phrase coupled with the subject, the verb remains the same. Ex: The manager, *accompanied by* his associates, *is* (not *are*) going to lunch.

according to: This phrase implies that the person to whom you're referring may not know — or be telling — the truth. If you don't want to give that impression, dump *according to* and use *said*.

active voice/passive voice: Active verbs require motion while passive verbs relate a state of existence. Active words energize your writing while passive verbs can sound wordy or indecisive. Ex: "My proposal *was* the best ever" sounds flat next to "I *proposed* a dynamite plan."

actually: See *virtually/actually*.

acumen: Means "keenness of mind" or "shrewdness."

ad: *Ad* is an abbreviation for *advertisement*. In formal language, use the entire word. If you abbreviate the word, don't use a period unless it's the end of the sentence.

adhere/cohere: *Adhere* refers to sticking together by gluing or grasping and *cohere* refers to parts of the same thing sticking together. Ex: Water molecules *cohere*. If you're referring to a cause or philosophy, use *adhere*.

adjacent/contiguous: In formal usage, *adjacent* means "lying near but not touching" while *contiguous* means "touching."

admission/admittance: *Admittance* refers only to the actual physical entry into a place. *Admission* has the extended meaning of acceptance into a group or organization.

advance/advanced: Anything in *advance* means that it is positioned in front or ahead, while someone or something that is *advanced* is higher in quality or caliber than the average.

advanced planning: See *plan ahead/advanced planning*.

advise/inform/write: In cover letters, a*dvise* is a pretentious way of saying *inform* or *write*. A cover letter is no place to offer advice to a prospective employer.

affect/effect: *Affect* means "to influence" and *effect* means "to make happen." Ex: The performance review *affected* my feelings; the *effect* was a joyous response.

aforementioned: Sounds pretentious. Use *this* or *that* instead.

agenda: Refers to a list of things to do. Use *agendas* for several lists.

ago/since: *Ago* means "earlier than the present time" and *since* means "from a definite past time to now." Never use these words together. Write "Ten years *ago* I..." or "It has been ten years *since* I..." not "It was ten years *ago since* I..."

ahold: This word is an inappropriate colloquialism. Use *get hold of*, *reach*, or *obtain*.

aid/aide: *Aid* refers to an action. Ex: My job is to *aid* Mike with the acquisition of new accounts. *Aide* refers to a person. Ex: Has my *aide* gone to lunch?

all ready/already: *All ready* means "completely ready" or "totally prepared." *Already* means "by this time" or "previously." Ex: "Are they *all ready* to go? They've *already* gone." Hint: Just write *ready* instead of *all ready*.

all right: Is spelled correctly. *Alright* is alwrong.

all-round: If you want to exhibit versatility, use *all-round*. If you're referring to "everywhere," *all-around* is more appropriate.

all the better: Is all the nicer when you know that using *all* with a superlative is perfectly OK.

allude/elude/refer: *Allude* implies an indirect relationship, while *refer* implies a direct relationship. Be careful to get this distinction right. *Elude* is unrelated to either *allude* or *refer*; it means to escape or avoid someone or something.

allusion/illusion: An *allusion* is a reference, usually indirect, to something else. *Illusion* is a false impression.

along: Commonly used to mean "approximately." Avoid this usage in formal correspondence and be more accurate. Ex: "I'll be there *along* about two" sounds foolish in comparison to "I'll be there at two."

along the lines of: Space waster. Substitute *like* instead.

along with: Means "as well as." When using this phrase, match the verb to the subject. Ex: Mike, along with his secretaries, *decides* (not decide) the weekly budget.

alot: Wrong! Write *a lot*.

a lot of: Used to mean "a great deal of," *a lot of* should be avoided in formal English. If you do use this phrase, make sure that the verb agrees with the word that follows. Ex: *A lot of* job seekers *write* cover letters, or *A lot of* time *is* spent looking for a job.

American: All too frequently, we use this phrase when we mean to say that an individual is a citizen of the United States. Remember that, when writing an international cover letter, saying what you really mean is better. You also avoid possibly alienating your Mexican or Canadian readers.

among/between: This distinction is an easy one to remember: use *among* when referencing more than three and *between* when discussing two.

another/additional: You can't use these words interchangeably. *Another* means "one more" and is specific to that meaning.

anxious/eager: Another pair that you should be careful of. *Anxious* has a sense of fear, doubt, or worry; *eager* means anticipating a joyous occasion.

arbitrate/mediate: In *arbitration* one person hears both sides of an issue and gives a binding decision. *Mediation* occurs when a person hears all information and tries to persuade the parties to come to a decision. A *mediator* has no binding power, though.

arrived at the conclusion that: Another wordy phrase that gets in your way. Go with, "I *concluded*." This phrase says what you mean and saves time.

as/because: In the sense of "due to the fact," *as* and *because* can be used interchangeably, but *as* tends to sound stuffy. You can confuse your reader, though, because *as* also refers to a point in time. Writing *because* is often better and also avoids potential problems.

as to whether: The *as to* is unnecessary. Just write *whether*.

at a later date: Save your reader time and write *later*.

at the present time/at the present writing: Both are stuffy ways of saying *now*. Say what you mean.

attached hereto/herein: The redundancy police are on their way to arrest you for this one. Say *attached* and save your record.

bachelor's: See *master's/bachelor's*.

bad: Too informal. Grab your thesaurus and replace *bad* with a good word.

become/get: Same meaning, different tone. *Become* has more class. Ex: "I *got* angry" sounds rash compared to "I *became* angry."

better than/more than: Both terms are used to mean *more than*, but *better than* is illogical. Ex: "She wrote *better than* 50 cover letters." *More than* is more accurate.

between/among: See *among/between*.

between every/between each: "A garage is *between each* office" literally means that a garage is situated in the middle of every office. Instead write, " a garage is *between every* two offices," or "a garage is *beside each* office."

between you and me: *Between you and I* is not grammatically correct. Without explaining all the confusing rules, try this quick trick: When in doubt, reverse the order of the objects — *between I and you* sounds ridiculous.

bit (with an adjective): Meaning "a small amount of," this word sounds immature in a cover letter. Ex: "Please spend a *bit* of time reading my resume."

bottom line: This near-cliché literally refers to the final line of a financial report, but it has evolved into a broader meaning of "the final result."

but: When used in place of "except," *but* is a preposition. If followed by a pronoun, use *me, her, him, us,* or *them.* Ex: "Nobody likes my cover letter *but me.*"

but/however, nevertheless: Using *but* may smooth your sentences. Using *however* or *nevertheless* formalizes your writing, but they may sound pretentious. If you're connecting two complete sentences, use a comma with *but* and a semicolon with the others. Never write *but however* — it's redundant.

but that/but what: While these terms are commonly used, they're unnecessarily wordy. Either use *that* alone or rework your sentence. Ex: Rather than writing "I don't doubt *but that* I can do the job," write "I don't doubt *that* I can do the job," or "I know I can do the job."

but (with a negative): Using *but* to mean *only* is awkward. Ex: "I received *but* four interviews." Replace *but* with *only* or revise the sentence.

can/may: *May* asks permission, while *can* expresses ability. A quick trick that helps is to rephrase the sentence using "have the ability." Ex: "*Can* I call you on Monday?" would read "Do I have the ability to call you on Monday?" I hope you do — what you need here is permission: "*May* I call you?"

cannot: Only separate this word (*can not*) when you want greater emphasis. Otherwise, "cannot" is all one word.

cannot but: "I *cannot but* be sorry." This phrase is too easily misunderstood. Can it but for everyday speech.

can't hardly: The correct form is *can hardly. Can't hardly* is not only grammatically incorrect, but it also has become associated with poor education in many regions.

can't help but: Dreaded double negative. Instead of saying, "You *can't help but* be impressed with me," write, "You *will* be impressed with me." See also *cannot but* and *can't hardly.*

capacity/ability: Where *ability* means competence in doing, *capacity* refers either to a position or duty or to the potential for storing. Don't use *capacity* to describe your skills. Ex: "I have the *capacity* to juggle many tasks at once" is incorrect.

capital/capitol: The only time to use *capitol* is when you are referring to the building that houses government, be it state or federal. Any other use should be *capital.*

cause/reason: A *cause* brings about an effect or result. A *reason* explains something.

city of. . .: Just name the city. "*City of* New Orleans" would be better as "New Orleans." Sorry, Arlo.

classy: An informal, but acceptable word for "stylish or elegant."

clever/ingenious/inventive: All mean varying degrees of "skillful or resource-ful." *Clever* implies mentally quick but lacking depth, *ingenious* refers to an ability to discover new solutions, and *inventive* requires imagination to produce something for the first time.

close proximity: Redundant. If something's *close*, it's in *proximity*. Use one or the other, never both.

close to the point of: Write *close to* and you'll be better off.

coach: Perfectly acceptable as a verb. Ex: "I *coached* her about interviews." Alternative words to use are *teach* or *instruct*.

cohere: See *adhere/cohere*.

cohese: Informal corruption of *cohere*. Do not use.

college: See *university/college*.

commend/praise: Another pair to be careful of. *Commend* should be used when you are talking about a specific action; *praise* is appropriate for generalities.

concerning the matter of: Hopeless bureaucrat speak. Write *concerning* or *about*.

consequent: See *subsequent/consequent*.

contiguous: See *adjacent/contiguous*.

continue on: Probably the most hated and annoying redundancy possible. If you want to make your reader's eyes bulge, *continue on* with this phrase. Otherwise, just say *continue*.

decided/decisive: While both mean "unquestionable or unmistakable," *decided* has the connotation of "definite," while *decisive* connotes "conclusive." Ex: "The company team won a *decisive* victory" or "A *decided* change has occurred in company policy."

definite/definitive: Both mean "unquestionable or decided" but *definitive* connotes "authority or finality."

despite/in spite of: Both are acceptable but *despite* is slightly more formal and eliminates wordiness. Using either word with *but* is unnecessary.

different from/than: Either form is acceptable, but *different from* is more accepted.

disclose/reveal: Should be used only when referring to confidential information that is being reported. Both mean "to make known," but if you want to connote a *sudden* disclosure, use *reveal* instead of *disclose*. Ex: "He opened the file and *revealed* that all of the cover letters had been stolen!"

discover/invent: *Discover* means to find something that already exists while *invent* means to produce something that has never existed before. These terms are not interchangeable.

discrete/discreet: These two may look like variations of each other, but they have separate meanings. *Discrete* means "distinct, unattached, unrelated," while *discreet* means "careful, considered."

discriminate/distinguish: While both words mean to discern or note difference, *discriminate* more specifically means to note difference and make a judgment accordingly.

disinterested/uninterested: These will get you in real trouble! *Disinterested* means "impartial"; while the person might be interested, she is unbiased. *Uninterested* means that the person is not at all concerned with what is going on. Say what you mean.

disregardless: Disregard this word. Use *regardless* instead.

divided into/composed of: These have almost opposite meanings. *Divided into* means that something that was originally together has been broken apart, and *composed of* means that the thing has been created out of separate parts.

double negatives: Use these and people will question your educational background. Ex: "I *didn't* send *no* cover letter." Make the sentence "I *didn't* send *a* cover letter." Words such as *scarcely*, *barely*, and *hardly* have negative connotations also, so don't pair them with a negative word.

double possessive: Although technically incorrect, double possessives are widely used and help to clarify possession. Ex: "We met through a friend of my father's" is clearer than "We met through a friend of my father."

double superlative: Using double superlatives (*most best, most fastest*), no matter how excited you are, is most unacceptable.

due to the fact that: Why all the extra words? Use *because* instead.

each: When *each* precedes a singular noun or is the subject of the sentence, use a singular verb. Ex: "*Each* cover letter *describes* my abilities perfectly" or "*Each is* perfect." When *each* follows a plural subject, use a plural verb. "They *each read* my cover letters for me."

each and every: Redundant and unnecessarily wordy. Avoid using this phrase unless you need the extra emphasis.

effect: See *affect/effect*.

e.g.: See *i.e./e.g.*

either/or: Look at the noun which follows *or*. If the noun is singular, use a singular verb, and if it's plural, use a plural verb. Ex: "Either my cover letters or my *resume needs* to be revised."

element/factor: An *element* is "a constituent part" of something else, while a *factor* is "something which actively contributes to the production of a result."

eliminate: To remove or eradicate. Do not use this word in place of *prevent*. Remember, you must have something to remove in order to eliminate it. Ex: I *eliminated* all wasteful expenditures.

else: Does not mean *or*. Ex: "You must send a resume *else* the employer won't know your qualifications" is wrong. Replace *else* with *or*. Watch for redundancy when using *else* with such words as *nobody* or *nothing*. In most cases, *else* can be omitted.

enclose/inclose: *Enclose* is more commonly used, but both words mean "to surround" and can be used interchangeably.

end result: A symptom of Redundancy Disease. Write simply *result*, omitting *end*.

enough: Commonly used for emphasis, *enough* is often redundant. Ex: I was happy *enough* that they invited me for an interview. This sentence sounds more sophisticated sans *enough*.

entirely completed: Is *entirely* redundant. *Completed* means to bring to an end — you won't find any degrees of completeness. Eliminate *entirely*.

equally as: *As* is used in comparing two or more elements to each other. Ex: I am *as* qualified *as* the other applicants. *Equally* is used when only one element of the comparison is named. Ex: My resume was *equally* good. If you have written *equally as*, delete *equally*.

especially/specially: Another important distinction. *Especially* has the sense of "particularly"; *specially* means that the event occurred for a specific reason. "I was *specially* trained for the task," but, "I am *especially* good at meeting budgets." See *more especially*.

-ess endings: In these PC days, avoid this ending to distinguish feminine subjects. Ex: *waitress, stewardess, actress.* Either use the nongender-specific term (*waiter, steward, actor*) or choose a different term (*food server, flight attendant, thespian*).

essential: Does not mean "very important," so don't write "My personality is *essential* for my success." Used correctly, *essential* means "necessary or indispensable." Ex: A well-written cover letter is *essential* for job search success. See *more essential.*

estimated at about: Once more redundancy raises its head. Leave out *about.*

every . . . and every: Even though this phrase seems to refer to many people or things, it takes a singular verb. Ex: *Every* resume *and every* cover letter *is* read with an open mind.

everybody/everyone: These words can be used interchangeably with one exception. *Every one* (two words) emphasizes each individual and cannot be replaced by *everybody.* In all cases, these words take a singular verb. Ex: *Everyone (Everybody) thinks* that my cover letter is brilliant, or *Every one* of my cover letters *is* a masterpiece.

everyday/every day: *Every day* indicates an event which occurs every 24 hours, or daily. Ex: I revise my cover letter *every day* at 5:00 pm. *Everyday* indicates a common occurrence, one which happens often, but not daily.

every other: This phrase can be confusing. I suggest you use *every day* or *every second day* to clarify your meaning.

ex-/former: Both are correct, but *former* is more formal. Ex: "She is a *former* lawyer" is more sophisticated than "she is an *ex*-lawyer."

exceed/excel: Both of these words mean "to go beyond," but they have different connotations. *Exceed* indicates that limits or expectations have been surpassed. Ex: I *exceeded* all sales expectations. *Excel* connotes superiority. Ex: I *excel* at sales performance.

extra: When used in place of "very" or "uncommonly," *extra* is too informal for a cover letter. Ex: My cover letter is *extra* long.

factor: See *element/factor.*

farther/further: When writing about a measurable distance, use *farther.* Ex: The bathroom is *farther* than the vending machines. When indicating an extension in time, use *further.* Ex: I will examine your resume *further.*

fewer in number: Keep your words fewer in number and write *fewer.*

fewer/less: When referring to individual items use *fewer*. Ex: I receive *fewer* than four interviews per month. When referring to a quantity or class of items, use *less*. Ex: *Less* jobs are available now.

figuratively/literally: These words cannot be used interchangeably. *Figuratively* means "metaphorically" while *literally* means "actually." Ex: He *figuratively* grabbed the bull by the horns and *literally* eliminated all wasteful expenditures.

file away: Don't make reading more work than it is by using two words where one will do. Write *file* and avoid finding your resume in the round file.

fiscal/monetary: *Fiscal* means "relating to financial matters" while *monetary* refers to money.

forego/forgo: *Forego* means to go before. *Forgo* (without the *e*) means to go without.

former: See *ex-/former* or *latter/former*.

for the purpose: Keep things simple and replace with *for* or *to*.

for the reason that: Overburdened way of saying *because*.

for your information: A quick and easy way to alienate the letter reader. Omit this phrase completely.

fractions: Numbers less than one should be written out. Ex: I received *two-thirds* of my sales experience overseas.

full time/full-time: When followed by a noun, hyphenate. Ex: I worked at *full-time* jobs through college. When it stands alone, do not hyphenate. Ex: I write cover letters *full time*.

gamut/gantlet/gauntlet: Often used interchangeably, these words have different meanings. *Gamut* refers to an entire range or series. Ex: My work experience covers the *gamut* from real estate to education. A *gantlet* is a flogging ordeal, and a *gauntlet* is a glove.

gather together: Redundant. If something is *gathered*, then it's *together*. Use one or the other.

get: See *become/get*.

group/team: Both words need singular verbs and pronouns, unless you've got more than one *group* or *team*. Ex: The *group/team is* aware of *its* problems.

he/she (the _____): Used as clarification, this phrasing is awkward and avoidable. Ex: The secretary told the CEO that *he* (the secretary) should get more rest. Without the clarification, the sentence is unclear as to who needs the rest, but with the clarification, the sentence is awkward. Revise it to read, The secretary told the CEO, "I need more rest."

he, him, his/she, her, hers/it, its/they, them, their, theirs: Always make sure that these *pronouns* agree with *their* subjects. As a test, replace the pronoun with the subject, then determine if the pronoun and subject agree in number. Ex: "*Everyone* took *their* places" is incorrect because *everyone* is a singular noun. The sentence should read "*Everyone* took *his* (or *her*) place".

he (she) is a man (woman) who: Ex: *He is a man who* commands respect. Why the extra words? Write "He commands respect."

he or she: Although some feminists may be angered, standard usage for a nongender-specific pronoun requires *he*. Ex: When someone sends a cover letter, *he* should follow up with a phone call. Writing *he or she* is cumbersome. If this practice really bothers you, try alternating the words *he* and *she*.

-ible: See *-able/-ible*.

idea: This word can encompass so many different meanings that choosing a more specific word, such as *design*, *belief*, *theory*, *hypothesis*, *solution*, *plan*, *objective,* is better — you get the idea?

i.e./e.g.: *i.e.* introduces a definition and *e.g.* introduces an example. Avoid these abbreviations in your cover letters and write "that is" or "for example."

if and when: Unnecessarily wordy and logically unsound. Use one or the other.

impel/induce: Because these definitions are similar, they are often used incorrectly as synonyms. *Impel* means to urge, force, or propel while *induce* means to persuade or influence. Ex: I *impel* you to read my cover letter. Hopefully, doing so will *induce* you to call me.

imply/infer: Here's an easy way to remember the distinction between these commonly confused words: The writer or speaker *implies* and the reader or listener *infers*.

important essentials: What other kind of *essentials* do you know of? Avoid this redundancy.

in accordance with your request: Cut the useless words; write *as you requested*.

in addition to: This wordy way of saying *also* does not change the verb. Ex: My resume, *in addition to* my cover letters, *positions* me as an aggressive candidate.

inasmuch as: Isspelledcorrectly. Don't separate the words. Better yet, choose a shorter alternative like *since* or *because*.

inclose: See *enclose/inclose*.

in connection with: Save ink! Write *about* or *concerning*.

in excess of: These excess words prevent concise writing. Try *more than* or *over* instead.

ingenious/inventive: See *clever/ingenious/inventive*.

in order to (that): In order to eliminate unnecessary words, just write *to*, *that*, or *so that*.

in respect to the matter of: You're using up too much space. Use *about* or *regarding*.

in spite of: See *despite/in spite of*.

intensives: Words such as *too, very, really, horribly, absolutely*, and *truly* are used to intensify statements. However, they've been *so* overused that instead of intensifying the interest, they now intensify the boredom. Avoid 'em.

in the amount of: When talking about money, writing *for* is clearer.

in the area of: Another roundabout way of saying *about*. Remember that specifics are better.

in the field of ... : Name your field rather than adding nothing words. Ex: "I have excelled *in the field of banking*," would be better with just *banking*.

in this day and age: Makes you sound really outdated. Replace with *now* or *today*.

in to/into: If you're expressing motion from one place to the inside of another, use *into*. Ex: I walked confidently *into* the room. When *in* and *to* are separated, motion towards an event or action is indicated. Ex: I walked confidently *in to* the interview.

invent: See *discover/invent*.

irregardless: *Irregardless* of how many times you've heard this word, it's wrong. Using it on a cover letter announces your ignorance of correct English. Write *regardless*.

its/it's: While apostrophes usually indicate possession, the rules change with pronouns. *Its* indicates possession. Ex: The cat got *its* claws trimmed. *It's* is a contraction for *it is*. The apostrophe replaces the missing *i*.

invaluable: Means priceless or valuable beyond estimation. If the value of something can be calculated, you cannot use this term.

join together: While beautiful in wedding ceremonies, this phrase is nevertheless redundant; you cannot *join apart*. Choose one word or the other.

juncture: While this term can be used to mean a point in time, it most accurately refers to a crisis or turning point.

keep continuing: Redundant. *Keep continuing* to use this phrase and you'll *keep continuing* to waste paper space.

kindly: Because this word means "in a kind manner," it doesn't convey the sense you want. Write instead, "Would you be so kind," or even, "please." As well, "I thank you *kindly*," would be best reworded as "I thank you *very much*."

kind of: Sounds like a kindergartner. Elevate your language; use *rather* or *somewhat* instead.

know/realize: Often used interchangeably, these words have slight differences in meaning. To *know* something is to have information or understanding. To *realize* something is to *know* it clearly or completely, to understand all aspects of it.

known to be: Means *is*. Use *is*.

know-how: Experts discourage the use of this word as too informal. Try *knowledge*, *understanding*, or *expertise* instead.

large portion of/large number of: These are weighty phrases that take up more room than you need to use. Replace with *most of* or *many*. Even better, though, would be to say *much*.

last/latest: These words are close in meaning but differ in connotation. *Last* connotes final, while *latest* means most recent.

last but not least: Should be buried; this phrase is too old for retirement.

latter/former: *Latter* refers to the second of two things, while *former* refers to the first. If you are discussing more than two objects, use *last-mentioned* or repeat the noun.

lay/lie: *Lay* means to put or place. *Lie* means to recline. To test your usage of these words, replace *lay* with *place*. If the sentence makes sense, use *lay*. If it doesn't, use *lie*.

less: See *fewer/less*.

like for: *For* gets in the way of what you mean. Simply write *like*.

like to have: Almost comically slang. Avoid in formal speech.

literally: See *figuratively/literally*.

lot/lots: Informal and unspecific. Tell us how many you mean.

love: Technically, this word refers to an intense affection or devotion, something cherished. Commonly, it has been used in so many contexts it has lost its singular meaning. Ex: "I *love* Disneyland" is probably an exaggeration. Experts suggest limiting your use of this word.

magnitude: An overblown word. Words like *importance*, *significance*, and *size* are more appropriate.

major: This adjective can only be used as a comparison. You can work on "*a* major account," but not "*the* major account."

manage: See *run/operate/manage*.

masterful/masterly: While you may be tempted to boast about your accomplishments, be careful in using these words. *Masterful* has the meaning of "strong or overbearing," while *masterly* means "with skill, expert in craft." Beware the wrong impression!

master's/bachelor's: That these are degrees in education is understood, so you can drop *degree*. Also, master's and bachlelor's are informal; the formal versions are Master of Arts/Science or Bachelor of Arts/Science.

maximize/minimize: *Maximize* means "to increase an object to its utmost potential," while *minimize* means the same in the other direction. Because of these extremes, you can't greatly, significantly, or vastly *maximize* or *minimize* anything.

may: See *can/may*.

memorandum: *Memorandum* is one piece of correspondence, while more than one can be either *memorandums* or *memoranda*. *Memorandas* is not accepted.

monetary: See *fiscal/monetary*.

more especially: Hopelessly redundant. Drop the *more*, and let *especially* do its job.

more essential: Face the facts: You're either *essential* or you're not, so you can't be *more essential*. Cut the redundant *more*.

more perfect: Too frequently, this phrase is another redundancy. Perfection cannot be measured in degrees.

more than/over: Use *over* when discussing large amounts as one concept: "*over* a million dollars," but *more than* in the case of things or people you have to count individually: "I wrote *more than* a thousand cover letters."

most certainly/most carefully: These phrases can show how earnest you are, but, more often than not, they sound pretentious.

mutual cooperation: Simply redundant. How else can you have cooperation? The same goes for *mutual teamwork*.

near future: Another redundancy. Conserve words and write "soon."

needless to say: This phrase is itself *needless to say*. Such a phrase suggests that you are just filling space.

neither/nor: Always use *nor* with *neither* to avoid being wrong.

never: Don't use *never* when you mean *not*. The two are not interchangeable. "The interviewer *never* mentioned salary during the interview," is not correct. Replace *never* with *not*.

new innovation: Yet another redundancy, this phrase is like writing "repeated again."

new record: Because a record is a new mark exceeding other achievements, *new record* is redundant.

nor: See *or/nor*.

not only/but also: This follow-phrasing requires that each element be comparable. "I *not only* require a comfortable working space *but also* good wages," would be better phrased, "I require *not only* a comfortable working space *but also* good wages."

nothing: *Nothing* always takes a singular verb: "My former employers may say that I am crazy, but *nothing is* further from the truth."

now pending: The redundancy disease strikes again! Now is the only time something can be *pending*.

of: This poor preposition is misused more than almost any other part of speech. The most common mistake occurs in using *of* when you really mean *have*. Should, would, could, must, and many more besides require the use of *have*. Ignore what it sounds like.

of between/of from: As far as numbers and dollar amounts are concerned, *between* and *from* are redundancies: "An increase in revenues *of between* five to eight million dollars," would be better written without the *between*.

official/officious: Another case in which you can give the wrong impression. *Official* means "one who is invested with an office," while *officious* means "overeager, meddlesome." Obviously, a mistake you don't want to make.

one of the, if not the: If you need to use this phrase, keep the elements in both: "I am *one of the* most important people, *if not the* most important." Often, you can get away with only the first part.

operate: See *run/operate/manage.*

optimize: A contender for the gold watch, *optimize* has been greatly overused in the last years. Use variants such as "increased efficiency" or "improved to maximum levels."

or/nor: If the negative quality of a sentence carries through the whole sentence, use *or.* "Don't use slang *or* profanity in cover letters." If the negative element ends or appears to end, use *nor*: "Don't use slang in an interview, nor should you arrive late for an interview."

outline in detail: See *spell out/outline in detail.*

over: See *more than/over.*

overall: This word is a candidate for retirement; it has been used too much and too often. Use words like *general, ultimate, comprehensive,* or *final.*

paramount: Another word that cannot be modified. This word means "chief" or "supreme," so you can't have something that is *more paramount* or *most paramount.*

passive voice: See *active voice/passive voice.*

past experience/past history: If you have experienced something or if something is history, it can be nowhere but past. Cut the redundancy.

per: You should only use this word within Latin phrases; otherwise, it sounds stuffy and pretentious. A good general rule is to simply avoid Latin or foreign phrases. Instead of *per diem* or *per annum,* use daily and yearly.

percent/percentage: The term *percent* is specific and requires a definite figure, while *percentage* needs some kind of modifier, like "large" or "significant."

period of: Another redundant phrase. Instead of writing, "I worked with the company for a *period of* six years," write simply, "I worked with the company *for* six years."

person/people: Use *persons* for an exact number of people: "I managed an office of eight *persons.*" The correct use of *people* is with a large crowd or an unknown amount.

personally: People too often use this word as an unnecessary introduction. Leave it out for the sake of clarity and conciseness. Anything that involves you is, by definition, personal.

perspective/prospective: *Perspective* is someone's point of view, while *prospective* is an expectation or a potentiality. An important detail in addressing a *prospective* employer.

plan ahead/advanced planning: The dreaded redundancy, once more. Wouldn't it be nice if we could plan for what has already happened?

please be advised: A pompous way of offering information or advice. A cover letter is no place to be pompous.

point in time: Another filler phrase. Write *now* instead.

practicable/practical: *Practicable* means that something can be done, while *practical* shows that something is worthwhile.

presently: This word means not only *now* but also *soon*. The best idea is to use the word that you really mean.

proceed/precede: *Proceed* means "to move forward" in any sense, not only for walking or real movement. *Precede* means "to go before," meaning something that occurred or came before something else.

proved/proven: Both are accepted, but *proved* is more common.

provided/providing: Don't use these words if you can replace them with the simple *if*.

purposely/purposefully: *Purposely* has the meaning "intentional," as in, "I *purposely* missed the board meeting." *Purposefully* has the sense of determination for reaching a goal. This is a commonly confused pair that you should be wary of.

qualified expert: Could you be an expert if you weren't qualified? Redundancy strikes again.

rather than: This phrase requires parallel verbs: "I quit *rather than* be fired" (not being fired).

real/really: *Real* means actual or true, while *really* means very. Be careful not to interchange the two.

realize: See *know/realize*.

reason: See *cause/reason*.

reason is because: Redundant. Rather than writing, "The *reason* I left the job *is because*," simplify the sentence to, "I left the job *because*." This redundancy is also true for *reason why*.

recommend/refer: A friend or contact *refers* you *to* a job offer. A firm or company is *recommended by* someone else. You would write, "Mr. A. *referred* me *to* this vacant position. Your company is highly *recommended by* the BBB."

regarding/concerning/respecting: These are all inflated words that can be replaced by the simple "about."

represent: A misleading word, *represent* can often be replaced by "composed" or "made up."

respectfully/respectively: *Respectfully* means "with respect," while *respectively* refers to objects and the order in which they occur in sentences. This error is an easy one to make, so watch out.

resume: See *vitae/resume*.

reveal: See *disclose/reveal*.

revert back: An obvious (or at least should be) redundancy. Avoid repetition.

run/operate/manage: *Run* is often used in place of *managed* or *operated*. A *manager* works for a boss, while an *operator* is usually the owner.

saving: When you use *a* with *saving*, the correct form is singular: "My programs resulted in *a saving* of millions," not *savings*.

scrutinize: Another word that is often attacked by redundancy. "A close scrutiny" and "to scrutinize closely" are both redundant.

seem: *Seem* is a wishy-washy word. Make a strong statement instead and show how determined you are.

seriously consider: If you ask a prospective employer to *seriously consider* your application, you are implying that his consideration isn't usually serious. Cut the *seriously* and lose the redundancy.

several: *Several* is ambiguous, but is pretty close to *few*. Use "many" or "numerous" for larger numbers. Even better, be specific.

since: See *ago/since*.

slanting: *Slanting* is when you intentionally avoid information that may damage your position. While slanting is not really lying, it can definitely be deceptive. You're better off to explain issues that might trip you up in a background check.

spell out/outline in detail: *Spelling out* means giving details, so this phrase is redundant. At the same time, though, *outlining* means summarizing, so this phrase is a contradiction.

state of the art: This phrase can be used either as a noun or an adjective; as an adjective, the phrase is hyphenated.

subject: When referring to people, *subject* is too vague. Spell out what you mean.

subject matter: *Subject* is usually enough. "The *subject matter* of the meeting centered on pay raises," can easily be rewritten without the *matter*.

subsequent/consequent: Easily mixed up words. *Subsequent* means "later" or "succeeding"; a *consequent* occurrence is something that naturally follows an action.

subsequent to: Inflated writing. Just use "after."

success: Because success is a positive thing, avoid writing "good success" or "beneficial success."

such: Avoid using *such* as an intensifier. In sentences like "It was *such* a hard job," rewrite using "very," or finish the comparison: "It was *such* a hard job that I needed extra money to finish it."

sufficient enough: Either word is strong enough on its own. Pairing them is redundant.

summarize: Use *summarize* only when you are giving a shortened version of a story.

summary: See above.

sure/surely: *Surely* is the adverb form; "I *sure* like working for you" is highly informal.

take for example: In most cases, *for example* is sufficient. To test, eliminate *take*. If the sentence still makes sense, you don't need *take*. Ex: *Take, for example*, cover letters are necessary in the job search. If you eliminate *take* from this sentence, it makes more sense.

take into consideration: Long-winded way of writing *consider*.

target: Is a fine word if it targets the meaning you want. However, *objective*, *goal*, or *quota* may hit the bullseye where *target* veers wide.

team: See *group/team*.

than: *Than* as a conjunction can take either "me" or "I" ("he" or "him," and so on) depending on the context. Finish the phrase to see which one to use; "The company pays Frank more than ... " can be finished with *me*, if the rest of the sentence is "they pay me," but can also be *I*, if the rest of the sentence is "I pay Frank."

than/then: The way to remember the difference here is to think of *then* as a mark of time and *than* as a comparison: "I worked for one manager for two years, *then* switched departments, but I liked the first department more *than* the second."

thank you in advance: Rude! Send a thank-you letter if you really mean it.

that (do you need it?): For brevity, try eliminating *that*. If the sentence still makes sense, great. Use "that" only for clarity. Ex: I read (*that*) cover letters are necessary. If you eliminate *that* here, the reader may initially misread the sentence.

that/which: An easy rule to remember: If the information following the word is necessary, use *that*. If the information is not necessary, use *which*. Ex: The cover letter, *which* is one of my best, got the manager's attention. *Which* introduces extra, not necessary, information. Ex: The cover letter *that* got the manager's attention was one of my best. In this case, the information following *that* is necessary to indicate which cover letter the writer is referring to.

there is, are, was, were: Weak construction. Revise your sentence. Ex: "*There are* two cover letters in the desk" can be rewritten as "Two cover letters are in the desk."

they: *They* say the word *they* is too general to be used in formal English. If possible, identify who *they* are. If you can't, rewrite your sentence to avoid the question, "Who is 'they'?"

thing: Undoubtedly, a more specific word exists. Avoid *thing*.

this/that/these/those: *These* words cannot stand on their own; they are not nouns. Always tell what you are referring to. Ex: *This* is great. What is great? *This* cover letter is great.

true facts: If they're not *true*, they're not *facts*. Avoid this redundancy.

try: Sometimes simple is better and *try* is a terrific word — brief and specific. But if you want more formality, you can use *attempt* (suggests a onetime event), *endeavor* (very formal, possibly pompous) or *strive* (connotes serious effort or energy).

try to/try and: *Try to* remember that *try and* is wrong. Think of it this way: To try *to* do something suggests one action while to try *and* do something suggests two actions, since *and* means in addition to. Ex: "*Try and* write a good cover letter," read literally, leads one to ask "What are you trying to do in addition to writing a cover letter?"

unfinished comparisons: "I'm the best!" Of what? Unless you're not willing to commit (advertisers often use this tactic so they don't have to prove their claim), always supply the comparison. Ex: I'm the best cover letter writer in the country. Then be prepared to back up your statement.

unique: Overused to the point of being meaningless, *unique* cannot be altered by comparative terms such as *more*, *very*, or *rather*. If something is *unique*, it should be the only one of its kind; therefore, nothing should exist to which it can be compared.

university/college: A *college* only awards undergraduate degrees, whereas a *university* awards master's and/or doctoral degrees as well.

unknown: Use this word only if what you are referring to is not known by anyone anywhere. If the thing may be known, use a more accurate word: *unidentified, undisclosed, unannounced, undetermined.*

unthinkable: If you have thought of something to declare *unthinkable*, then you have thought of it; therefore, it is not *unthinkable*, but very unlikely, impossible, or un-do-able. A more accurate description is thinkable.

up to date/up-to-date: If this phrase refers to a noun which follows it, use hyphens. Ex: Only send *up-to-date* cover letters. If the phrase stands alone, don't use hyphens. Ex: Never send cover letters that are not *up to date*.

valued/valuable: *Valuable* refers to something that costs a great deal. *Valued* refers to something (or someone) that is held in high regard, whether or not it's *valuable*. People cannot be *valuable*, but they can be *valued*. Ex: I am a *valued* employee.

very: OK in "thank you *very* much" but very, very, very overused as a superlative. Avoid this word when possible.

vice: When used preceding a noun, do not use a hyphen. Ex: *vice president, vice chairperson, vice principle.*

virtually/actually: Do not mean the same thing. *Virtually* means almost entirely, while *actually* means in fact or in truth. An easy way to remember: *Actually* is and *virtually* almost is.

vis-à-vis: Although many people use this word to mean about or concerning, its correct definition is "in relation to" or "as compared with." Ex: How do you feel about your cover letters now, *vis-à-vis* the first cover letters you wrote?

vitae/resume: A *resume* is not the same as a *vitae*. A *vitae* is a brief biographical sketch whereas a *resume* is a summary of your skills and employment history. Where *resumes* typically do not run more than two pages, some curricula *vitae* run more than 50 pages. For more information see my book *Resumes For Dummies*.

want/wish: While these words are correctly used as synonyms, *wish* usually refers to a desire for something abstract or remote and *want* refers to more available, tangible desires. Ex: I *want* to work for you. I *wish* I could make two billion dollars a year.

was a former: Redundant. Either use *was* alone or write *is a former*.

way in which: Too wordy. Eliminate *in which* and use that saved space to write something brilliant.

we: How can such a little, simple word cause any problems? When we don't know who *we* refers to. Ex: In my company, *we* attend meetings weekly. Who is *we*? Everyone? Almost everyone? Everyone but the secretaries? Be specific.

whatsoever at all: *Whatsoever* means the same thing as *at all*. Why for what reason use both together?

which: See *that/which*.

while: When used in place of *although*, be alert to possible misunderstanding. Ex: *While* I received most of my education from the University of Brazil, I got my professional experience in California and Canada. Use *although* for greater clarity.

who/whom: *Who* is a subject and *whom* is an object. Doesn't help? Think of it this way: Turn the sentence in question into a question and answer it with *he* (*she, they*) or *him* (*her, them*). If the answer is *he*, then use *who* in the sentence. If the answer is *him*, use *whom*. Ex: Tell me *who/whom* she called. Rephrased as a question: *Who* did she call? The answer: She called *him*. Since the answer is *him*, the original sentence should read: Tell me *whom* she called.

whoever/whomever: See *who/whom* and follow the same procedure.

who's/whose: When in doubt, replace with *who is* or *who has*. If the sentence makes sense, use *who's*. If it doesn't, use *whose*.

wide-: In most cases, *wide-* preceding a noun needs a hyphen. Ex: *wide-awake, wide-ranging, wide-screen*. For ultimate surety, up look the word in question up in a dictionary.

-wide: Behind the noun, no hyphen. Ex: *nationwide, companywide, worldwide*.

-wise: If it means smart, use a hyphen. Ex: *street-wise, money-wise.* If it means "in regard to," then drop the hyphen. Ex: *otherwise, lengthwise, crosswise.* Beware of creating *-wise* words, such as *performancewise, saleswise,* or *moneywise.* Casewise, other choices wordwise are more appropriate contextwise. Write intelligently, not -wisely.

with the exception of: *With the exception of* this sentence, this phrase is too wordy. Replace it with *except* or *except for.*

worthwhile/worth while: Here's an easy trick: Stick *your* or *one's* in between *worth* and *while.* If it makes sense, use *worth while.* If it doesn't, use *worthwhile.* Better yet, choosing a more specific description is *worth while,* such as *promising* or *worth your time.*

yet: It's only three letters, yet it takes up space. Only use this word for clarity. If a sentence makes sense without *yet,* delete it. Ex: Have you written a cover letter (*yet*)?

you know: No, I don't. Why don't you tell me? Use this tired, illogical revision of *um* and you look like a hesitant teenager, you know?

your/you're: The quick rule: Replace with *you are.* If the sentence makes sense, use *you're.* If it doesn't, use *your.*

yours/your's: *Your's* does not exist. Use *yours.*

zeal/zest: *Zeal* refers to an ardent interest in pursuit of something. *Zest* refers to a keen enjoyment or gusto. Ex: I have a *zest* for writing cover letters. I *zeal*ously want to write better cover letters.

Index

The Fun & Easy Way™ to learn about computers and more!

10/31/95

Windows® 3.11 For Dummies® 3rd Edition
by Andy Rathbone

ISBN: 1-56884-370-4
$16.95 USA/
$22.95 Canada

Mutual Funds For Dummies™
by Eric Tyson

ISBN: 1-56884-226-0
$16.99 USA/
$22.99 Canada

DOS For Dummies® 2nd Edition
by Dan Gookin

ISBN: 1-878058-75-4
$16.95 USA/
$22.95 Canada

The Internet For Dummies® 2nd Edition
by John Levine & Carol Baroudi

ISBN: 1-56884-222-8
$19.99 USA/
$26.99 Canada

Personal Finance For Dummies™
by Eric Tyson

ISBN: 1-56884-150-7
$16.95 USA/
$22.95 Canada

PCs For Dummies® 3rd Edition
by Dan Gookin & Andy Rathbone

ISBN: 1-56884-904-4
$16.99 USA/
$22.99 Canada

Macs® For Dummies® 3rd Edition
by David Pogue

ISBN: 1-56884-239-2
$19.99 USA/
$26.99 Canada

The SAT® I For Dummies™
by Suzee Vlk

ISBN: 1-56884-213-9
$14.99 USA/
$20.99 Canada

Here's a complete listing of IDG Books' ...For Dummies® titles

Title	Author	ISBN	Price
DATABASE			
Access 2 For Dummies®	by Scott Palmer	ISBN: 1-56884-090-X	$19.95 USA/$26.95 Canada
Access Programming For Dummies®	by Rob Krumm	ISBN: 1-56884-091-8	$19.95 USA/$26.95 Canada
Approach 3 For Windows® For Dummies®	by Doug Lowe	ISBN: 1-56884-233-3	$19.99 USA/$26.99 Canada
dBASE For DOS For Dummies®	by Scott Palmer & Michael Stabler	ISBN: 1-56884-188-4	$19.95 USA/$26.95 Canada
dBASE For Windows® For Dummies®	by Scott Palmer	ISBN: 1-56884-179-5	$19.95 USA/$26.95 Canada
dBASE 5 For Windows® Programming For Dummies®	by Ted Coombs & Jason Coombs	ISBN: 1-56884-215-5	$19.99 USA/$26.99 Canada
FoxPro 2.6 For Windows® For Dummies®	by John Kaufeld	ISBN: 1-56884-187-6	$19.95 USA/$26.95 Canada
Paradox 5 For Windows® For Dummies®	by John Kaufeld	ISBN: 1-56884-185-X	$19.95 USA/$26.95 Canada
DESKTOP PUBLISHING/ILLUSTRATION/GRAPHICS			
CorelDRAW! 5 For Dummies®	by Deke McClelland	ISBN: 1-56884-157-4	$19.95 USA/$26.95 Canada
CorelDRAW! For Dummies®	by Deke McClelland	ISBN: 1-56884-042-X	$19.95 USA/$26.95 Canada
Desktop Publishing & Design For Dummies®	by Roger C. Parker	ISBN: 1-56884-234-1	$19.99 USA/$26.99 Canada
Harvard Graphics 2 For Windows® For Dummies®	by Roger C. Parker	ISBN: 1-56884-092-6	$19.95 USA/$26.95 Canada
PageMaker 5 For Macs® For Dummies®	by Galen Gruman & Deke McClelland	ISBN: 1-56884-178-7	$19.95 USA/$26.95 Canada
PageMaker 5 For Windows® For Dummies®	by Deke McClelland & Galen Gruman	ISBN: 1-56884-160-4	$19.95 USA/$26.95 Canada
Photoshop 3 For Macs® For Dummies®	by Deke McClelland	ISBN: 1-56884-208-2	$19.99 USA/$26.99 Canada
QuarkXPress 3.3 For Dummies®	by Galen Gruman & Barbara Assadi	ISBN: 1-56884-217-1	$19.99 USA/$26.99 Canada
FINANCE/PERSONAL FINANCE/TEST TAKING REFERENCE			
Everyday Math For Dummies™	by Charles Seiter	ISBN: 1-56884-248-1	$14.99 USA/$22.99 Canada
Personal Finance For Dummies™ For Canadians	by Eric Tyson & Tony Martin	ISBN: 1-56884-378-X	$18.99 USA/$24.99 Canada
QuickBooks 3 For Dummies®	by Stephen L. Nelson	ISBN: 1-56884-227-9	$19.99 USA/$26.99 Canada
Quicken 8 For DOS For Dummies® 2nd Edition	by Stephen L. Nelson	ISBN: 1-56884-210-4	$19.95 USA/$26.95 Canada
Quicken 5 For Macs® For Dummies®	by Stephen L. Nelson	ISBN: 1-56884-211-2	$19.95 USA/$26.95 Canada
Quicken 4 For Windows® For Dummies® 2nd Edition	by Stephen L. Nelson	ISBN: 1-56884-209-0	$19.95 USA/$26.95 Canada
Taxes For Dummies™ 1995 Edition	by Eric Tyson & David J. Silverman	ISBN: 1-56884-220-1	$14.99 USA/$20.99 Canada
The GMAT® For Dummies™	by Suzee Vlk, Series Editor	ISBN: 1-56884-376-3	$14.99 USA/$20.99 Canada
The GRE® For Dummies™	by Suzee Vlk, Series Editor	ISBN: 1-56884-375-5	$14.99 USA/$20.99 Canada
Time Management For Dummies™	by Jeffrey J. Mayer	ISBN: 1-56884-360-7	$16.99 USA/$22.99 Canada
TurboTax For Windows® For Dummies®	by Gail A. Helsel, CPA	ISBN: 1-56884-228-7	$19.99 USA/$26.99 Canada
GROUPWARE/INTEGRATED			
ClarisWorks For Macs® For Dummies®	by Frank Higgins	ISBN: 1-56884-363-1	$19.99 USA/$26.99 Canada
Lotus Notes For Dummies®	by Pat Freeland & Stephen Londergan	ISBN: 1-56884-212-0	$19.95 USA/$26.95 Canada
Microsoft® Office 4 For Windows® For Dummies®	by Roger C. Parker	ISBN: 1-56884-183-3	$19.95 USA/$26.95 Canada
Microsoft® Works 3 For Windows® For Dummies®	by David C. Kay	ISBN: 1-56884-214-7	$19.99 USA/$26.99 Canada
SmartSuite 3 For Dummies®	by Jan Weingarten & John Weingarten	ISBN: 1-56884-367-4	$19.99 USA/$26.99 Canada
INTERNET/COMMUNICATIONS/NETWORKING			
America Online® For Dummies® 2nd Edition	by John Kaufeld	ISBN: 1-56884-933-8	$19.99 USA/$26.99 Canada
CompuServe For Dummies® 2nd Edition	by Wallace Wang	ISBN: 1-56884-937-0	$19.99 USA/$26.99 Canada
Modems For Dummies® 2nd Edition	by Tina Rathbone	ISBN: 1-56884-223-6	$19.99 USA/$26.99 Canada
MORE Internet For Dummies®	by John R. Levine & Margaret Levine Young	ISBN: 1-56884-164-7	$19.95 USA/$26.95 Canada
MORE Modems & On-line Services For Dummies®	by Tina Rathbone	ISBN: 1-56884-365-8	$19.99 USA/$26.99 Canada
Mosaic For Dummies® Windows Edition	by David Angell & Brent Heslop	ISBN: 1-56884-242-2	$19.99 USA/$26.99 Canada
NetWare For Dummies® 2nd Edition	by Ed Tittel, Deni Connor & Earl Follis	ISBN: 1-56884-369-0	$19.99 USA/$26.99 Canada
Networking For Dummies®	by Doug Lowe	ISBN: 1-56884-079-9	$19.95 USA/$26.95 Canada
PROCOMM PLUS 2 For Windows® For Dummies®	by Wallace Wang	ISBN: 1-56884-219-8	$19.99 USA/$26.99 Canada
TCP/IP For Dummies®	by Marshall Wilensky & Candace Leiden	ISBN: 1-56884-241-4	$19.99 USA/$26.99 Canada

'or scholastic requests & educational orders please all Educational Sales at 1. 800. 434. 2086

FOR MORE INFO OR TO ORDER, PLEASE CALL ▶ 800 762 2974

For volume discounts & special orders please call Tony Real, Special Sales, at 415. 655. 3048

Title	Author	ISBN	Price
The Internet For Macs® For Dummies® 2nd Edition	by Charles Seiter	ISBN: 1-56884-371-2	$19.99 USA/$26.99 Canada
The Internet For Macs® For Dummies® Starter Kit	by Charles Seiter	ISBN: 1-56884-244-9	$29.99 USA/$39.99 Canada
The Internet For Macs® For Dummies® Starter Kit Bestseller Edition	by Charles Seiter	ISBN: 1-56884-245-7	$39.99 USA/$54.99 Canada
The Internet For Windows® For Dummies® Starter Kit	by John R. Levine & Margaret Levine Young	ISBN: 1-56884-237-6	$34.99 USA/$44.99 Canada
The Internet For Windows® For Dummies® Starter Kit, Bestseller Edition	by John R. Levine & Margaret Levine Young	ISBN: 1-56884-246-5	$39.99 USA/$54.99 Canada

MACINTOSH

Title	Author	ISBN	Price
Mac® Programming For Dummies®	by Dan Parks Sydow	ISBN: 1-56884-173-6	$19.95 USA/$26.95 Canada
Macintosh® System 7.5 For Dummies®	by Bob LeVitus	ISBN: 1-56884-197-3	$19.95 USA/$26.95 Canada
MORE Macs® For Dummies®	by David Pogue	ISBN: 1-56884-087-X	$19.95 USA/$26.95 Canada
PageMaker 5 For Macs® For Dummies®	by Galen Gruman & Deke McClelland	ISBN: 1-56884-178-7	$19.95 USA/$26.95 Canada
QuarkXPress 3.3 For Dummies®	by Galen Gruman & Barbara Assadi	ISBN: 1-56884-217-1	$19.99 USA/$26.99 Canada
Upgrading and Fixing Macs® For Dummies®	by Kearney Rietmann & Frank Higgins	ISBN: 1-56884-189-2	$19.95 USA/$26.95 Canada

MULTIMEDIA

Title	Author	ISBN	Price
Multimedia & CD-ROMs For Dummies® 2nd Edition	by Andy Rathbone	ISBN: 1-56884-907-9	$19.99 USA/$26.99 Canada
Multimedia & CD-ROMs For Dummies® Interactive Multimedia Value Pack, 2nd Edition	by Andy Rathbone	ISBN: 1-56884-909-5	$29.99 USA/$39.99 Canada

OPERATING SYSTEMS:

DOS

Title	Author	ISBN	Price
MORE DOS For Dummies®	by Dan Gookin	ISBN: 1-56884-046-2	$19.95 USA/$26.95 Canada
OS/2® Warp For Dummies® 2nd Edition	by Andy Rathbone	ISBN: 1-56884-205-8	$19.99 USA/$26.99 Canada

UNIX

Title	Author	ISBN	Price
MORE UNIX® For Dummies®	by John R. Levine & Margaret Levine Young	ISBN: 1-56884-361-5	$19.99 USA/$26.99 Canada
UNIX® For Dummies®	by John R. Levine & Margaret Levine Young	ISBN: 1-878058-58-4	$19.95 USA/$26.95 Canada

WINDOWS

Title	Author	ISBN	Price
MORE Windows® For Dummies® 2nd Edition	by Andy Rathbone	ISBN: 1-56884-048-9	$19.95 USA/$26.95 Canada
Windows® 95 For Dummies®	by Andy Rathbone	ISBN: 1-56884-240-6	$19.99 USA/$26.99 Canada

PCS/HARDWARE

Title	Author	ISBN	Price
Illustrated Computer Dictionary For Dummies® 2nd Edition	by Dan Gookin & Wallace Wang	ISBN: 1-56884-218-X	$12.95 USA/$16.95 Canada
Upgrading and Fixing PCs For Dummies® 2nd Edition	by Andy Rathbone	ISBN: 1-56884-903-6	$19.99 USA/$26.99 Canada

PRESENTATION/AUTOCAD

Title	Author	ISBN	Price
AutoCAD For Dummies®	by Bud Smith	ISBN: 1-56884-191-4	$19.95 USA/$26.95 Canada
PowerPoint 4 For Windows® For Dummies®	by Doug Lowe	ISBN: 1-56884-161-2	$16.99 USA/$22.99 Canada

PROGRAMMING

Title	Author	ISBN	Price
Borland C++ For Dummies®	by Michael Hyman	ISBN: 1-56884-162-0	$19.95 USA/$26.95 Canada
C For Dummies® Volume 1	by Dan Gookin	ISBN: 1-878058-78-9	$19.95 USA/$26.95 Canada
C++ For Dummies®	by Stephen R. Davis	ISBN: 1-56884-163-9	$19.95 USA/$26.95 Canada
Delphi Programming For Dummies®	by Neil Rubenking	ISBN: 1-56884-200-7	$19.99 USA/$26.99 Canada
Mac® Programming For Dummies®	by Dan Parks Sydow	ISBN: 1-56884-173-6	$19.95 USA/$26.95 Canada
PowerBuilder 4 Programming For Dummies®	by Ted Coombs & Jason Coombs	ISBN: 1-56884-325-9	$19.99 USA/$26.99 Canada
QBasic Programming For Dummies®	by Douglas Hergert	ISBN: 1-56884-093-4	$19.95 USA/$26.95 Canada
Visual Basic 3 For Dummies®	by Wallace Wang	ISBN: 1-56884-076-4	$19.95 USA/$26.95 Canada
Visual Basic "X" For Dummies®	by Wallace Wang	ISBN: 1-56884-230-9	$19.99 USA/$26.99 Canada
Visual C++ 2 For Dummies®	by Michael Hyman & Bob Arnson	ISBN: 1-56884-328-3	$19.99 USA/$26.99 Canada
Windows® 95 Programming For Dummies®	by S. Randy Davis	ISBN: 1-56884-327-5	$19.99 USA/$26.99 Canada

SPREADSHEET

Title	Author	ISBN	Price
1-2-3 For Dummies®	by Greg Harvey	ISBN: 1-878058-60-6	$16.95 USA/$22.95 Canada
1-2-3 For Windows® 5 For Dummies® 2nd Edition	by John Walkenbach	ISBN: 1-56884-216-3	$16.95 USA/$22.95 Canada
Excel 5 For Macs® For Dummies®	by Greg Harvey	ISBN: 1-56884-186-8	$19.95 USA/$26.95 Canada
Excel For Dummies® 2nd Edition	by Greg Harvey	ISBN: 1-56884-050-0	$16.95 USA/$22.95 Canada
MORE 1-2-3 For DOS For Dummies®	by John Weingarten	ISBN: 1-56884-224-4	$19.99 USA/$26.99 Canada
MORE Excel 5 For Windows® For Dummies®	by Greg Harvey	ISBN: 1-56884-207-4	$19.95 USA/$26.95 Canada
Quattro Pro 6 For Windows® For Dummies®	by John Walkenbach	ISBN: 1-56884-174-4	$19.95 USA/$26.95 Canada
Quattro Pro For DOS For Dummies®	by John Walkenbach	ISBN: 1-56884-023-3	$16.95 USA/$22.95 Canada

UTILITIES

Title	Author	ISBN	Price
Norton Utilities 8 For Dummies®	by Beth Slick	ISBN: 1-56884-166-3	$19.95 USA/$26.95 Canada

VCRS/CAMCORDERS

Title	Author	ISBN	Price
VCRs & Camcorders For Dummies™	by Gordon McComb & Andy Rathbone	ISBN: 1-56884-229-5	$14.99 USA/$20.99 Canada

WORD PROCESSING

Title	Author	ISBN	Price
Ami Pro For Dummies®	by Jim Meade	ISBN: 1-56884-049-7	$19.95 USA/$26.95 Canada
MORE Word For Windows® 6 For Dummies®	by Doug Lowe	ISBN: 1-56884-165-5	$19.95 USA/$26.95 Canada
MORE WordPerfect 6 For Windows® For Dummies®	by Margaret Levine Young & David C. Kay	ISBN: 1-56884-206-6	$19.95 USA/$26.95 Canada
MORE WordPerfect 6 For DOS For Dummies®	by Wallace Wang, edited by Dan Gookin	ISBN: 1-56884-047-0	$19.95 USA/$26.95 Canada
Word 6 For Macs® For Dummies®	by Dan Gookin	ISBN: 1-56884-190-6	$19.95 USA/$26.95 Canada
Word For Windows® 6 For Dummies®	by Dan Gookin	ISBN: 1-56884-075-6	$16.95 USA/$22.95 Canada
Word For Windows® For Dummies®	by Dan Gookin & Ray Werner	ISBN: 1-878058-86-X	$16.95 USA/$22.95 Canada
WordPerfect 6 For DOS For Dummies®	by Dan Gookin	ISBN: 1-878058-77-0	$16.95 USA/$22.95 Canada
WordPerfect® 6.1 For Windows® For Dummies® 2nd Edition	by Margaret Levine Young & David Kay	ISBN: 1-56884-243-0	$16.95 USA/$22.95 Canada
WordPerfect® For Dummies®	by Dan Gookin	ISBN: 1-878058-52-5	$16.95 USA/$22.95 Canada

10/31/95

The Internet For Macs® For Dummies® Quick Reference
by Charles Seiter

ISBN:1-56884-967-2
$9.99 USA/$12.99 Canada

Windows® 95 For Dummies® Quick Reference
by Greg Harvey

ISBN: 1-56884-964-8
$9.99 USA/$12.99 Canada

Photoshop 3 For Macs® For Dummies® Quick Reference
by Deke McClelland

ISBN: 1-56884-968-0
$9.99 USA/$12.99 Canada

WordPerfect® For DOS For Dummies® Quick Reference
by Greg Harvey

ISBN: 1-56884-009-8
$8.95 USA/$12.95 Canada

Title	Author	ISBN	Price
DATABASE			
Access 2 For Dummies® Quick Reference	by Stuart J. Stuple	ISBN: 1-56884-167-1	$8.95 USA/$11.95 Canada
dBASE 5 For DOS For Dummies® Quick Reference	by Barrie Sosinsky	ISBN: 1-56884-954-0	$9.99 USA/$12.99 Canada
dBASE 5 For Windows® For Dummies® Quick Reference	by Stuart J. Stuple	ISBN: 1-56884-953-2	$9.99 USA/$12.99 Canada
Paradox 5 For Windows® For Dummies® Quick Reference	by Scott Palmer	ISBN: 1-56884-960-5	$9.99 USA/$12.99 Canada
DESKTOP PUBLISHING/ILLUSTRATION/GRAPHICS			
CorelDRAW! 5 For Dummies® Quick Reference	by Raymond E. Werner	ISBN: 1-56884-952-4	$9.99 USA/$12.99 Canada
Harvard Graphics For Windows® For Dummies® Quick Reference	by Raymond E. Werner	ISBN: 1-56884-962-1	$9.99 USA/$12.99 Canada
Photoshop 3 For Macs® For Dummies® Quick Reference	by Deke McClelland	ISBN: 1-56884-968-0	$9.99 USA/$12.99 Canada
FINANCE/PERSONAL FINANCE			
Quicken 4 For Windows® For Dummies® Quick Reference	by Stephen L. Nelson	ISBN: 1-56884-950-8	$9.95 USA/$12.95 Canada
GROUPWARE/INTEGRATED			
Microsoft® Office 4 For Windows® For Dummies® Quick Reference	by Doug Lowe	ISBN: 1-56884-958-3	$9.99 USA/$12.99 Canada
Microsoft® Works 3 For Windows® For Dummies® Quick Reference	by Michael Partington	ISBN: 1-56884-959-1	$9.99 USA/$12.99 Canada
INTERNET/COMMUNICATIONS/NETWORKING			
The Internet For Dummies® Quick Reference	by John R. Levine & Margaret Levine Young	ISBN: 1-56884-168-X	$8.95 USA/$11.95 Canada
MACINTOSH			
Macintosh® System 7.5 For Dummies® Quick Reference	by Stuart J. Stuple	ISBN: 1-56884-956-7	$9.99 USA/$12.99 Canada
OPERATING SYSTEMS:			
DOS			
DOS For Dummies® Quick Reference	by Greg Harvey	ISBN: 1-56884-007-1	$8.95 USA/$11.95 Canada
UNIX			
UNIX® For Dummies® Quick Reference	by John R. Levine & Margaret Levine Young	ISBN: 1-56884-094-2	$8.95 USA/$11.95 Canada
WINDOWS			
Windows® 3.1 For Dummies® Quick Reference, 2nd Edition	by Greg Harvey	ISBN: 1-56884-951-6	$8.95 USA/$11.95 Canada
PCs/HARDWARE			
Memory Management For Dummies® Quick Reference	by Doug Lowe	ISBN: 1-56884-362-3	$9.99 USA/$12.99 Canada
PRESENTATION/AUTOCAD			
AutoCAD For Dummies® Quick Reference	by Ellen Finkelstein	ISBN: 1-56884-198-1	$9.95 USA/$12.95 Canada
SPREADSHEET			
1-2-3 For Dummies® Quick Reference	by John Walkenbach	ISBN: 1-56884-027-6	$8.95 USA/$11.95 Canada
1-2-3 For Windows® 5 For Dummies® Quick Reference	by John Walkenbach	ISBN: 1-56884-957-5	$9.95 USA/$12.95 Canada
Excel For Windows® For Dummies® Quick Reference, 2nd Edition	by John Walkenbach	ISBN: 1-56884-096-9	$8.95 USA/$11.95 Canada
Quattro Pro 6 For Windows® For Dummies® Quick Reference	by Stuart J. Stuple	ISBN: 1-56884-172-8	$9.95 USA/$12.95 Canada
WORD PROCESSING			
Word For Windows® 6 For Dummies® Quick Reference	by George Lynch	ISBN: 1-56884-095-0	$8.95 USA/$11.95 Canada
Word For Windows® For Dummies® Quick Reference	by George Lynch	ISBN: 1-56884-029-2	$8.95 USA/$11.95 Canada
WordPerfect® 6.1 For Windows® For Dummies® Quick Reference, 2nd Edition	by Greg Harvey	ISBN: 1-56884-966-4	$9.99 USA/$12.99/Canada

For scholastic requests & educational orders please call Educational Sales at 1. 800. 434. 2086

FOR MORE INFO OR TO ORDER, PLEASE CALL ▶ 800 762 2974

For volume discounts & special orders please call Tony Real, Special Sales, at 415. 655. 3048

3/26/96

IDG BOOKS WORLDWIDE™

Order Center: **(800) 762-2974** *(8 a.m.–6 p.m., EST, weekdays)*

Quantity	ISBN	Title	Price	Total

Shipping & Handling Charges

	Description	First book	Each additional book	Total
Domestic	Normal	$4.50	$1.50	$
	Two Day Air	$8.50	$2.50	$
	Overnight	$18.00	$3.00	$
International	Surface	$8.00	$8.00	$
	Airmail	$16.00	$16.00	$
	DHL Air	$17.00	$17.00	$

*For large quantities call for shipping & handling charges.
**Prices are subject to change without notice.

Ship to:

Name _____

Company _____

Address _____

City/State/Zip _____

Daytime Phone _____

Payment: ☐ Check to IDG Books Worldwide (US Funds Only)

☐ VISA   ☐ MasterCard   ☐ American Express

Card # _____ Expires _____

Signature _____

Subtotal _____

CA residents add
applicable sales tax _____

IN, MA, and MD
residents add
5% sales tax _____

IL residents add
6.25% sales tax_____

RI residents add
7% sales tax_____

TX residents add
8.25% sales tax_____

Shipping_____

Total _____

Please send this order form to:
**IDG Books Worldwide, Inc.
Attn: Order Entry Dept.
7260 Shadeland Station, Suite 100
Indianapolis, IN 46256**

*Allow up to 3 weeks for delivery.
Thank you!*